Aberdeenshire Library and Information Service
www.aberdeenshire.gov.uk/libraries
Renewals Hotline 01224 661511

D0808441

2 9 DEC 2

1 3 JAN 2011

2 1 JUL 2011

2 8 APR 2012

- 3 MAY 2014
2 7 JUN 2014

1 7 JAN 2015

ABERDEENSHIRE
LIBRARY &
INFORMATION SERVICES

WITHDRAWN
FROM LIBRARY

DUDLEY, Jill

Ye gods! II

ALIS

2666510

YE GODS!

II

JILL DUDLEY

MORE TRAVELS IN

GREECE

ABERDEENSHIRE LIBRARY AND INFORMATION SERVICES	
2666510	
HJ	2538738
914.95	£7.99
AD	ANF

Published by
Orpington Publishers
Email: info@orpingtonpublishers.co.uk

Origination by
Creeds the Printers,
Broadoak, Dorset.
01308 423411

Cover design
and illustration by
Clare E. Taylor

Printed by
J. H. Haynes & Co. Ltd.
Sparkford, Yeovil.
01963 440 635

Copyright © Jill Dudley 2008

ISBN 10: 0-9553834-2-0
ISBN 13: 978-0-9553834-2-7

CONTENTS

INTRODUCTION

Ye Gods! II is a follow up to Ye Gods! It is a mixture of pagan and Christian legends, and my own fascination with how Christianity took over from the old Olympian gods and absorbed certain things from the pagan past.

Those who in my earlier books have come to love Harry and sympathize with his dilemma of trying to keep up with me, can follow him again and either laugh or feel pity.

As always, our travels take us to ancient temple sites, to monasteries and to early Byzantine churches. We travel overland by bus or taxi, or we take ferry-boats. Each journey has been a sort of pilgrimage.

CHAPTER

1

ELEUSIS

As on previous occasions when flying in to Athens and approaching Greek god territory, I expected some sort of revelation to hit me, but nothing mystic happened.

That first night Harry and I had dinner on the roof-garden of our hotel surrounded by terracotta pots of orange trees and jasmine. From there we watched night descend over Athens. We overlooked the Acropolis which loomed black and appeared very like a bombed site, until suddenly the flood-lighting of the Parthenon made it resplendent and totally majestic against the night sky. Things were looking good, even if the flickering candle on our table failed to give the adequate light Harry liked to have when eating foreign dishes.

The next day was set aside to visit the great sanctuary of Demeter, goddess of corn and agriculture, far out in the suburbs of Athens. When we caught the bus the passengers eyed us as we took our seats. We hadn't punched our tickets - well, we had no tickets to punch supposing, as in London, we would be sold them on the bus. We should have bought them earlier and felt quite pleased with our ignorance whilst we thought we'd get away with it. Unfortunately, it wasn't long before an inspector came on board. There was no way to correct the mistake - all passengers are supposed to buy tickets in advance from kiosks dotted about the pavements of Athens.

I held money out to him. "English," I said in Greek, and explained that we hadn't travelled on an Athens bus before and didn't know the customs of his country. The inspector paid no attention to my excuses and began to write. I appealed to the passengers, but they averted their eyes as soon as they caught me looking at them. The inspector's face remained impassive as he passed us our two fines and waited for payment. Reluctantly we handed over the money.

With great civility, a kindly Greek businessman asked us where we wanted to go. When I told him Eleusis, he did all he could to help. Greeks always appear to treat lost travellers as though they have been sent to test them. Was this businessman hoping by his kindness that we two toads of English would reveal ourselves quite suddenly as royalty?

First he showed us where to get off the bus and took us immediately to buy tickets; then he led us down into the underground, boarded a train with us and escorted us off again. He next accompanied us across what seemed to be half a dozen busy thoroughfares, and took us to a bus station where he found out the precise time of our bus, helped us to buy tickets, and showed us exactly where to wait for it. Finally, he shook hands, showed no sign of disappointment that we didn't suddenly appear with crowns and sceptres, and proceeded on his way to catch a ferry for the islands.

My first Greek textbook had in it lengthy exercises in the present tense about how it was the custom for Greeks at the weekend '...to go to an island where the family has a large house. There they sun-bathe and swim and in the evenings, if the weather is hot and the moon is out, they sing and dance...' Such are the things one learns from a textbook; but nowhere does it mention that the people of the country put themselves out so completely in order to help travellers. That is something foreigners learn for themselves.

There was nothing Sacred about the Way as our bus rattled along through the suburbs of Athens. After many enquiries as to whether we'd arrived, and patient reassurances that we would be told when to get off; after passing factory buildings, depots and warehouses, we drove into ever worse industrialization with cement and petro-chemical plants, huge factory chimneys and gas-works. This was the modern reality of the ancient Sacred Way from Athens to Eleusis. Eventually we saw the sea on our left, and passed cargo quays, giant cranes, wharfs, rusty container ships and whatnot.

The bus stopped. Eleusis, we were told. I remembered the words of our hotel receptionist who'd looked surprised when I'd asked her how to get to this place. "Why you wish to go, to meet friends?" "No, to see the ancient sanctuary," I'd answered. The girl had shrugged and looked at us pityingly. "Two minutes there and it is enough," she'd remarked. I had returned her look with an equally pitying one; clearly she had no sense of history, no idea of the past glories of her country, no imagination.

"Where are we?" Harry asked. He never really knows where we are going when abroad, and is completely foxed by foreign place names.

"Eleusis. The wonderful and marvellous sanctuary of Demeter, goddess of corn," I replied, trying to stir up some enthusiasm in this god- or rather goddess-forsaken location. "As a farmer you'll be interested."

The sanctuary was a hundred yards or so inland, enclosed within a perimeter fence. At first glance there was nothing to see but ruins, paved and weedy terraces and fallen column drums, backed by its acropolis at the foot of which was a cave.

I pointed to the cave and said to Harry: "That's the entrance to the underworld." Before its dark and menacing entrance a group of students sat chatting and drinking cans of Coke.

As we began wandering around I told Harry the Demeter legend. Apparently, Hades, god of the underworld, had one day seen Demeter's daughter, the beautiful Persephone, picking wild flowers in a meadow, and had snatched and dragged her screaming to the deep halls of his subterranean kingdom. Poor Demeter, unaware of what had happened and anguished by her daughter's disappearance, searched the world for her. In time she learned from the sun that Zeus, supreme god of the ancient world, had given her as bride to Hades. Eventually, Demeter came to Eleusis where, disguised as an old crone in mourning, she sat beside the Kallichoron Well and refreshed herself with its water. We ourselves were now beside the well. We found a couple of convenient rocks to sit on.

I tried to cast myself back into antiquity, to understand Demeter's grief and capture Harry's imagination with the story. I told him how at the time there'd been a king and queen of Eleusis who'd had three daughters. One day the daughters came to the well and, finding the mourning goddess in disguise, took her home to the palace where she was welcomed by the queen and taken on as nurse to her baby son. The goddess loved the child, and fed him on ambrosia (the food of the gods) but by night she secretly held him in the hearth so he was wrapped in flames which, rather surprisingly, was supposed to immortalize him. One night the queen in horror caught her doing this.

"Are you listening still?" I asked Harry whose eyes I noticed were beginning to glaze over. The shock to his system of travelling, after the quiet solitude of farm life, always exhausted him.

"Carry on," he said. Clearly he was listening or he wouldn't have noticed my question.

"On being discovered, Demeter rather carelessly dropped the baby who, not unnaturally, began to scream."

"It didn't kill him?" (He was listening).

"No, he was partially immortalized, remember? Demeter then threw off her disguise and showed herself to the queen as the great goddess she was, whose actions were done only out of love."

"So, what about it?" Harry's dismissal of the myth was an insult to the legend, or my ability to tell the story and convey its symbolism. I said firmly: "It was the whole point of the Eleusinian Mysteries, that's what about it!" And I told him how the baby, having achieved partial immortality thanks to Demeter, was much like Persephone who was doomed to die to the upper world and yet return to life.

"So what about Persephone?" Harry was still alert enough to be aware I hadn't told him the whole story.

"I'm coming to it," I said, and told him the legend as recorded in Homer's Hymn to Demeter. How, when the king learned Demeter was a goddess, he immediately set about building a temple in her honour. But, as long as she could find no trace of her daughter, Demeter continued to mourn, and abandoned her worldly duties to the point that everything withered and died, and men were on the verge of extinction. "The world was in such straits," I went on, "that the gods of Olympus themselves were suffering because they received no sacrifice. Realizing that without men - without men, mind you! - there was absolutely no point to the existence of gods, Zeus ordered his brother Hades to release Persephone to the upper world to put an end to all the dying and withering."

"And did he?"

"Yes, but not before Hades got her to eat a pomegranate seed which, in this instance, was the food of the dead. This meant that she could only remain for two thirds of the year above ground, and one third had to be spent with Hades. A sort of annual resurrection and, I suppose, a reflection of the immortality part of the story."

I looked across at the ruins of what must once have been a magnificent sanctuary with columns and statues and which, without the surrounding concrete houses for today's industrial workers, would have had a view to the sea and the island of Salamis. To the north of the precinct was the dark mouth of the cave, with the group of students still seated in front of it. There at its entrance had once been a small temple of Hades known as the Ploutoneion. I pointed to the cave. "Can you imagine Persephone being dragged screaming down through there, and then, I suppose, coming back up in the spring, all smiles?"

"I can't imagine anything" came the reply.

I ignored his dismissal, and went on: "When her daughter reappeared, Demeter was so overjoyed that immediately the land blossomed, the grass grew and, most importantly, there were once again fields of standing corn."

"Makes a good bedtime story," Harry agreed, his eyes beginning to close. But I ignored the signs of sleep and told him how, with the reappearance of her daughter, Demeter informed the king of her secret rites which were to be divulged only to those initiated into her cult. From then on the Eleusinian Mysteries were to be celebrated annually, and were to continue for over two thousand years.

A couple of women with earnest faces, dressed in long flowing cotton skirts and sandals, were wandering nearby. They had the aloof air of literary highbrows, and were engrossed in some discussion, snatches of which I could catch.

"But I know...Orfefs...brought back Evrydike - " (In Greek 'eu' is pronounced 'ef').

"...Orpheus and Eurydice like everyone..."

"...also Odysefs..."

"You're doing it again!"

"Not convinced...ask her."

I looked behind me for the 'her' and saw the speaker meant me.

"The poor man's asleep. Anyway, she probably won't know." They passed by, two superior beings wrapped in their world of thought.

I left Harry in his own underworld of sleep and tried to make sense of the ruins as I made my way through them. Before I'd come out to Greece I'd read about a professor, E.D. Clarke, who at the beginning of the nineteenth century thought he'd found the cult figure of Demeter at Eleusis. It rose out of a dung heap beside the Lesser Propylaea (entrance gates). The interesting thing about the statue was that the locals at that time had complete faith in this 'cult figure' for the success of their harvests, but now addressed it as Agia Demetria (Saint or Holy Demetria).

E.D. Clarke, like Lord Elgin with the Parthenon marbles, had been determined to bring the statue back to England. He'd defied all local protest, and organized its transport. It was regarded as a particularly ill omen when, on the eve of its removal, an ox went berserk and butted at the statue before galloping away, bellowing and trampling the corn of the Rharian plain. The Orthodox priest, ignoring local belief that anyone removing the statue would find his arm wither or drop off, bravely wielded the first blow with a pickaxe in order to help prise it from its base. Nothing calamitous happened to his arm, and the statue was eventually dislodged and trundled on rollers down to the sea where it was put on board a ship for England. The ship, however, foundered off Beachy Head and it was only by great effort and persistence that Clarke managed to get the cult statue raised from the sea bed. It was finally taken to its new destination, the Fitzwilliam Museum, Cambridge, where it is now on view as one of the museum's valued exhibits.

Although the professor believed it to be Demeter's cult statue (having been guided in this by ancient records and literary sources), later scholars declared it to be no such wonder, but one of the caryatid figures which had stood either side of the Lesser Propylaea.

Cult figure or not, the strange fact remains that everywhere in the vicinity of Eleusis is now concrete and tarmac, whilst all around Cambridge are to be seen prairie like fields of standing corn. Interesting!

Most Greek sanctuaries were open to all who wanted to honour the god or goddess. Demeter, however, had her secret rites and, before anyone could share in her celebrations, he or she had to be initiated into her Mysteries. Men, women and children, as well as slaves, were eligible on condition they spoke Greek; it was imperative also that the candidate was of good character. If those wanting initiation were acceptable, then they first had to attend what were known as the Lesser Mysteries in Athens, held in the early spring in a temple of Demeter and Kore (Persephone) beside the bank of the Ilissos river, east of the Acropolis.

The Greater Mysteries were held in the autumn and lasted nine days. They began with the Kistai (the sacred things of Demeter) being carried in procession from Eleusis to Athens where they were deposited in Demeter's Eleusinion at the foot of the Acropolis on its north-west side. The arrival in Athens of the great goddess of corn was then announced to Athena's priestess.

Early in the morning of the second day the initiates were called by heralds to go down to the sea for purification. They took with them young pigs which they purified before sacrificing them to the goddess. After the sacrifice the pigs were buried deep in the ground as an offering to the gods of the underworld.

The following two days of the Greater Mysteries were given over to prayers and blessings. Then, on the fifth day, a spectacular procession set out from Athens bearing the sacred things of Demeter back to her sanctuary at Eleusis, a distance of some ten miles. At some stage along the route a wooden statue of the seldom heard of god Iacchos joined the procession; Iacchos is believed to have been an epiphany of Dionysos, god of wine and drama. The statue bore a torch, and was crowned with a wreath of myrtle; it was placed in a carriage and was accompanied by the priest of Iacchos.

One of the resting places for the procession was the ancient temple of Daphnaios Apollo, midway between Athens and Eleusis. The temple was destroyed by the Christians in the fifth century A.D. in order to build a basilica church. Today the site is marked by the superb Monastery of Daphni which has taken its name in a truncated form from the earlier temple of Apollo Daphnaios. Only one column remains of the original temple, and few visitors are aware of the site's former importance.

Before the procession reached Eleusis, led by Iacchos and the priests and priestesses of Demeter, a narrow bridge had to be crossed. Here there was a rather odd custom. Awaiting the procession on the other side of the bridge were men with their heads covered to conceal their identity. They first allowed the priests and priestesses and the sacred things of Demeter to pass, then hurled abuse and insults at the V.I.Ps who followed. These dignitaries were expected to endure these taunts in silence; it was a humbling exercise intended to remind those in high office to guard against arrogance, and any inclination towards self-aggrandisement.

The procession finally arrived at Eleusis after dark with the initiates bearing torches. There the role of Iacchos seems to have ended as he disappears from the scene. Despite the ten mile walk, and despite fasting, the evening ended with singing and dancing around the Kallichoron Well.

I soon found myself beside the Telesterion, the ancient temple site of Demeter. It had, apparently, been unlike any other Greek temple. There were shallow steps mounting to its terrace, and the peak of the temple roof had had in it a hole, or sort of chimney, from which a holy fire had erupted. Plans for it had been drawn up by Ictinus, the architect responsible for the Parthenon, no less. Very little is known about what actually happened there because the initiates were sworn to secrecy. What has been gleaned has come from inscriptions, archaeological discoveries, and from literary sources.

It is known, for instance, that on one of the days there had been the Dromena (a sacred pageant). The pageant told the story of the abduction of Persephone, and the misery as Demeter searched the world for her, before the final joy of their reunion.

I could imagine the numerous columns which had been a feature of the temple; they must have given an added mystique to the scene. During the Dromena, the darkness had been pierced by bright flashing illuminations with shadowed tableaux, whilst the High Priest intoned the story of Persephone's descent to the dark and fearful halls of Hades. From where I stood the mouth of the cave was visible beyond. When the return of Persephone was proclaimed, an enormous gong was sounded, the sort used in Greek dramas to simulate thunder.

But it was the great erupting fire which appeared through the hole in the temple roof which was of significance. The Hierophant had a throne close to this fire, and when it erupted he proclaimed: 'The Mistress has given birth to a holy boy, Brimo has given birth to Brimos! that is, the Strong One to the Strong One.'

Well, it was anybody's guess what all this meant, but presumably it represented Demeter holding the queen's baby son in the flames in order to immortalize him.

Finally, the most sacred and secret things (known as the

Hiera) were revealed by the High Priest. What these secret things were has never been revealed. The second century Christian theologian, Clement of Alexandria, did his best to denigrate the Eleusinian Mysteries and, with the Hiera in mind, declared that he blushed even to think of it; but, as he was never initiated, and it had remained a profound secret on penalty of death if it was ever revealed, it was clearly in his Christian interests to infer the 'secret things' were the lewdest and most obscene objects imaginable.

At some point in the final stages of the pageant, when the priest was portraying the terrors of Persephone's descent into the underworld, an ear of corn was held up in a moment of profound silence, symbolizing eternal life and resurrection.

I supposed when Christianity had come along it had been an exciting idea for mortals to be told things were no longer merely an ear of corn symbolizing resurrection, but that now all could expect literally to rise up to heaven.

Harry, when I'd discussed this with him once, had told me to stop speculating. When I died, he warned, if God existed, I'd be better off having made an effort at some semblance of belief than not. I shouldn't make light of what was an eternal irreversible destiny. Supposing everything was true, he'd warned?

That was a sobering thought. Supposing it was!

But if all was a matter of faith, had pagan belief been any the less true to pagans then, than Christianity to believing Christians now?

"Of course! No. Yes. Oh, I don't know," came Harry's answer when I'd put the question.

I thought that the Greater Mysteries coming from Athens to Eleusis must have been rather like the Easter celebrations in the Greek Orthodox Church today. After the sorrow expressed at the Good Friday services, and the evening's candle-light procession with tolling bells and general mourning, there was Christ's Resurrection bringing great joy. Shortly before midnight, at this latter celebration, the lights of all the churches are extinguished and, on the stroke of midnight, the priest in the darkened sanctuary comes forward bearing a single lighted candle, the new 'Light of the world', and proclaims triumphantly 'Christos anestei!' ('Christ is risen!')

I'd once been told by the assistant to the Orthodox Archbishop in London, that this 'Light' was actually brought to Athens from the Holy Fire which is believed to miraculously ignite itself every year at the Resurrection service within the Holy Sepulchre (Christ's tomb) in Jerusalem. Because of the time difference between Israel and Greece, this flame is able to be flown in and used for the new 'Light of the world' in Athens. I thought it sounded unlikely, but it was what I was told. Was there, I wondered, any similarity between the fire in the Holy Sepulchre and the former fire in the Anaktoron (the holy of holies) in Demeter's temple at Eleusis?

The two women were approaching and I could hear them talking.

"No, Diana, it was definitely here that Persephone - "

"But I can promise you, Beryl, that in Sicily I've seen a similar cave."

"No matter. She reappeared at this Ploutoneion where Hades had his temple - his only temple, I believe."

Both at the same moment smiled as they wandered up. They didn't introduce themselves but the Diana woman remarked: "Beryl's been reminding me about the passage in St. Paul's first letter to the Corinthians which referred directly to the worshippers of Demeter. Demeter had a temple at Corinth, you know."

The Beryl woman said: "The passage in St. John's Gospel 12:24 is even more persuasive: '...unless a grain of wheat falls into the earth and dies, it remains alone; but if it dies, it bears much fruit.'"

"How interesting!"

"There is so much connection! So much significance in everything!" said the Diana woman. She went on: "Tell her about the Omphalos, the umbilical cord conjoining new life with the old."

"Yes, they say there was an Omphalos stone here like they had at Delphi," said her companion. "It's all so interesting!" She stood in silence staring towards Harry asleep beside the Kallichoron Well.

She turned to me and said: "People don't come to this place unless they are studying the ancient gods and their worship. We're wondering if you have a special interest here?"

"My interest is in Christian absorption of pagan customs and festivals," I said.

"How very fascinating." And, instead of their eyes appearing politely vacant like some people's did when I told them this, they seemed genuinely to want to hear more.

"And have you found many links?" asked the Diana woman.

"Well, it all began on my first visit to Greece when I noticed there were many Orthodox saints who had the same names, or ones similar to the old pagan gods," I said.

"So intriguing!" said the Beryl woman. "Agios Demetrios, I expect was one of them?"

"Of course! And, then there's Agios Dionysios - one iota different from the god Dionysos. Really, there are very many with slight variations, or sometimes saints with the epithets of the gods, such as St. George from Zeus Georgios, meaning 'of the earth' and so on."

"Endless fascination!" agreed the Beryl woman.

"Beryl's main interest lies with pagan death and resurrection," said the other with a nod of acknowledgment at her friend.

"Symbolism and resurrection," explained the Beryl woman. "The ankh in Egyptian hieroglyphs, symbolic of eternal life, so similar to the Christian cross which became the labarum used by Constantine after he'd seen the vision in the sky."

"And heard the voice saying 'By this sign conquer'," said the other.

"Then there's Persephone who ate a pomegranate seed which condemned her to return to Hades but allowed her resurrection for two thirds of every year. So symbolic!"

"The time it takes for germination to take place," said her companion.

"Yes. And without death there can be no resurrection," said the Beryl woman with the unswerving conviction of a luminary.

"Can't there?" I asked.

"Think about it!" said the woman nodding sagely at me.

They both watched me attentively, as though some intelligent remark was expected. But I was beginning to feel dizzy with the one and then the other batting their balls of information at me.

"I'll give it some thought later," I said.

One of them looked at her watch and drew the attention of her companion to the time. I noticed also that Harry was surfacing from the depths of oblivion.

"Well, it's been nice talking to you," I said. "You've really helped bring this place to life for me."

"Enjoy the rest of your time here," said the one.

"Maybe we'll meet again," said the other.

"Though really it isn't likely as we're leaving now. We're driving to Parga - "

"On the north-west coast - quite a drive."

"We're wanting to see the nearby Nekromanteion - " said the Beryl woman.

"Oracle of the dead," whispered the Diana woman.

"Another entry to Hades where the tragedy of Orfefs and Evrydike - "

"Orpheus and Eurydice," explained the whisper.

"Was said to have taken place. We fly back from Kerkyra - "

"Corfu," smiled the whisper with a nod.

With that we parted, and I was left ruminating about Agios Demetrios and the goddess Demeter, and the cult or non-cult statue addressed as Agia Demetria on which fields of standing corn had seemed to depend.

Amazingly, the cult of the goddess Demeter had been so great and of such importance that, far from dying out when Christianity began to spread, there had been ever increasing numbers of initiates, and the buildings at Eleusis had had to be enlarged to receive them all. It wasn't until four hundred years after Christ that the Mysteries had stopped - not fourteen or forty or one hundred, but four hundred! And it wasn't because of the conversion of the masses, the sudden enlightenment of the people, but because the Emperor Theodosius the Great closed down all sanctuaries and forbade pagan worship and sacrifice.

Harry joined me. "How much longer are we having to stay in this God-forsaken dump?" he asked.

What sacrilege!

"Dump? This isn't a dump, it's a sacred oasis in a God-forsaken industrial eyesore," I replied. "You have to look at it through the eyes of those who lived two thousand years ago."

"That's all gone. Now is now, not millennia ago."

We left the cave and terrace of the ancient temple, and made our way up its acropolis behind to have a picnic under a pine tree. Several thin cats sat around and waited with extreme patience and politeness for whatever food we could spare.

Once it must have been beautiful looking from this vantage point over the sanctuary's marble buildings and colonnades and the great entrance, to the sparkling sea and the island of Salamis beyond. There the Persian fleet had been defeated at the great naval battle of Salamis. It was said that it was due to the mystical power of Eleusis that the Athenian army had triumphed. Apparently, two men had seen a swirl of dust rising from Eleusis, as if made by some thirty thousand men, and at the same time had heard the sound of voices. One of the men knew it was the sound of the mystical 'Iacchos' and explained to his companion, who was a stranger to the rites performed at Eleusis, that this unearthly cry came from Eleusis to aid the Athenians. Yes, miracles had happened in the name of the gods, just as today there are miracles in the name of the saints.

But today at Eleusis the only dust raised in the air is from tall factory chimneys puffing pollution to the skies. Now there is only tarmac and concrete sprawling across the land instead of corn fields. I took a photograph, defying Harry's 'What on earth do you want to take that for?'

"Just for the record," I said.

And I took another, and another, and just one more in

case the others failed. After all, it had once been one of the most important sites of the ancient world.

2

EPIDAURUS

We were half an hour into our journey from Athens to the Peloponnese when I noticed our plump-faced bus driver's eyelids growing heavy. I looked away and hoped for the best. A little later I glanced at him again and saw his head down on his chest.

What should one do when a driver is seen sleeping at the wheel, jump up and shout 'oy'? Or go forward and have a quiet word in his ear? An icon of a saint and a medallion of the Virgin Mary kept the bus on course, with no veering to left or right, as we sped along the Athens-Corinth highway. Greek music blared, and buff curtains fluttered by the open windows.

For some obscure reason Harry didn't seem too bothered when I told him. When abroad he never likes to cause a fuss, and never speaks to foreigners if he can avoid it. Suddenly I saw the driver's head jolt up, and the eyelids spring up like blinds on windows. It had only been a short nap. He turned up the radio, and strident voices, accompanied by bouzoukis, filled the bus with a lament;

Greek music tends to reflect the harsh lives of a people who have always had to battle with the elements, or free themselves from foreign domination or, in this case, fight to stay awake to stay alive.

The bus rattled over the Corinth Canal, that masterpiece of engineering connecting the Gulf of Corinth with the Saronic Gulf. Not long afterwards we stopped and a group of Greek peasant women clambered on board. I saw an old crone bowed with age and thought she surely wouldn't travel on the bus; but she was heaved up like a small black bundle. Because there was no seat, Harry offered her his and she sat down beside me.

I expected her to smell, but she was perfectly laundered and washed and sat very quietly by my side. Her capable looking daughter stood nearby keeping a watchful eye. Despite my limited Greek I offered her a sweet, hoping to start up a conversation. "Thelete?" I enquired. She turned her black shawled head up and I found myself looking down into the brightest eyes I had ever seen in a deeply wrinkled face. She happily put out a gnarled hand and took a sweet. In Greek I told her I was on holiday and that I loved Greece, and that was my husband who had given her his seat. He was a farmer, I said, and had forty cows. I hoped I had the word for 'cows' right and hadn't said 'angels', as the words were somewhat similar. To my surprise she seemed to understand, but when she herself began to speak I was unable to unravel a word; there was absolutely no comprehension on my part, and I despaired of making headway with the language. The capable daughter smiled understandingly.

They didn't stay long on the bus. When she got off a rough gypsy-looking woman elbowed her way past the passengers, and seized the seat beside me. She had a hard weather-beaten face. I offered her a sweet also but she shook her head dismissively and crossed herself. In fact she crossed herself repeatedly at every wayside shrine and every church and signpost. It seemed a sort of reflex action like touching wood; or else a safety measure left over from the ancient past when travellers would pay their respects to pillars of stone at cross-roads known as 'Hermae'. These had served to remind travellers of the god Hermes (guardian of souls and travellers). In Roman times he was Mercury, and in the Christian era he became identified with the Archangel Michael who guided the souls of the dead and who, in early Christian art, bore the attributes of Hermes, such as a broad-brimmed hat and a wand. In the Orthodox Church today the priest recites, 'For an Angel of peace; a faithful Guide, a Guardian of our souls and bodies, let us entreat the Lord.'

It was September and the countryside from Corinth to Argos was typical of Greece, with its back-cloth of grey mountains, its foreground of olive and orange groves, dried river-beds and dusty roads. In due course we saw the sea in the distance, sparkling blue and serenely calm in the afternoon sun. We arrived at our destination at about three in the afternoon.

Naufplion is a picturesque town of Venetian influence. From the balcony of our small hotel close to the bus station, we overlooked an alleyway. Lines of tables, covered by bright chequered cloths, were placed before the narrow houses with their wrought iron balconies. Behind them towered the Venetian fortress of Palamidhi.

From the diners in the alleyway that first night came a cacophony of voices: the high strident ones of Greek women, the strong, assertive ones of men, and the shrill piping of children, all mingling with the loud guttural guffaws from parties of Germans recounting anecdotes. These human voices were occasionally overshot by fights between screaming cats. The human chatter lasted until two in the morning, after which only the intermittent yowling of cats and the chiming of clocks interrupted sleep, each clock striking ten minutes after the other like repeater alarms.

I was aware that what had been a mere suspicion of toothache was becoming worse with every passing hour, a reminder that a visit to the dentist was long overdue. I couldn't trace it to any particular tooth, and had several well-filled molars in the area where it ached. I took a couple of pain-killers and clenched my jaws on a swab dipped in whisky which, after a while, calmed things down.

I fell into a restless sleep at dawn, only to be awoken by early morning greetings from the alleyway: 'Yeia sou, Eleni!' 'Yeia sou, Ioannis!' 'Yeia sou, Maria! Ti kaneis?' (Health to you! How are you?) Apart from my tooth problem I was very well, thank you. I put a pillow over my head.

Later that morning, as we waited for a bus to take us to Epidaurus, the ancient centre of healing, Harry said: "Toothache? Where?"

"Where do you suppose?"

"Let me look."

But I wasn't going to stand at the bus stop with my mouth wide open.

"You don't want toothache, not out here in Greece," Harry remarked. "God knows what their hygiene's like - ooooof! It doesn't bear thinking of!" I could expect nothing less from Harry who was only voicing my own anxieties. I wasn't keen to go to anyone who might get bonuses for pulling teeth.

"You might get Aids," Harry went on unhelpfully. "It's why dentists wear rubber gloves in case their patients bite them."

The subject was dropped abruptly, and my problem was totally eclipsed when we unexpectedly witnessed an accident. A young man setting off on his motorbike was accelerating away when his pillion passenger, unready for the unexpected momentum of it, fell off backwards. He had no helmet and, as his head hit the road, there was a crunch as his neck gave way.

"Oh, God!"

"Poor devil! That's him gone!"

We were about to rush to his assistance when, to our relief, this tall young man got up, gave us a sheepish grin, and climbed back onto the motorbike as though the whole episode had been a public stunt for our entertainment. In a moment, the two had set off again without a care in the world.

We were left very much aware of the infinitesimally fine line drawn between good fortune and happiness, and ill fortune with its miserable consequences. What protector had placed a hand beneath his head to lessen the blow? In ancient Athens a new-born infant underwent a ritual for his future safety. It was important for him to be put under the care of Hestia, goddess of the hearth and guardian of the home and family. It was the custom then for a new-born child to be carried at the run around the domestic hearth, considered to be the centre of the home. Today an infant in the Orthodox Church is plunged three times in the baptismal water, following which he is carried three times around the font, and put under the protection of a saint.

Soon we were on our way, this time driven by a young man who'd acquired the skill of driving with his elbows, leaning on the steering wheel in a very relaxed manner. How relaxed could a driver get, I wondered? Well, he could fall asleep, I supposed.

Epidaurus was a gently spectacular site situated in a plain surrounded by mountains. Its tranquil setting seemed to envelop the visitor with a feeling of peace. Here it was that in the past incurables had come in the expectation of a miracle. Pain, when you suffer from it, is a lonely, solitary matter which no one else can share or draw away from you. You are sucked into a vortex with it, and there is no escape until it's gone. An onlooker can imagine it but remains an outsider, an observer only.

"Tooth all right?" asked Harry kindly.

I would have preferred not to have been reminded of it. I felt precariously poised between signs of improvement and impending calamity. My jaw felt stiff and, if things got worse, I wondered if I'd be able to open my mouth enough for inspection. What could a dentist do about that?

"I expect our insurance will cover a dentist. Lucky you speak Greek," Harry said brightly. "But a Greek dentist! Ow!"

I was determined not to spoil the day with 'scenarios', and told Harry firmly that all symptoms had gone. I changed the subject to the history of the site. No one had been allowed to die within the sanctuary precincts, I informed him, which I supposed was a sort of comfort. Neither had a woman been allowed to give birth, come to that. Legend had it that it was at Epidaurus that the god Asclepius had been born, conceived by Apollo on a mortal woman who had then exposed the baby on a nearby mountainside. A shepherd found the infant and, recognizing its divinity by the light which glowed about him (much like the light about Jesus depicted in nativity scenes) he took the baby home. There Asclepius was cared for and protected by the shepherd's dog, and suckled by his goat.

Later the child was taught the art of medicine by Chiron, a Centaur who was half man, half horse. Chiron was renowned throughout the ancient world for his medical knowledge, his music and his justice.

"His powers of healing became so great," I said, "that Asclepius even raised somebody - Hippolytus, son of Theseus, in fact - from the dead. But, unlike God when Jesus raised Lazarus, when Asclepius raised Hippolytus Zeus was so furious with him for going against the laws of nature, that he flung a thunderbolt at Asclepius and killed him. This in turn outraged Apollo, who immediately killed the Cyclopes who'd made the thunderbolt. Anyway, because Asclepius was the son of Apollo, he wasn't really killed but was somehow immortalized by way of apotheosis."

"Apotheosis? Hum."

"It means he was deified and became both man and god."

The toothache was definitely ebbing which made me feel quite bright again. I told Harry how at Epidaurus the sick would spend the night in the Abaton, a building in the vicinity of the temple of Asclepius, where it was expected that during the night each patient would be visited by the god himself, or would receive a curative remedy in a dream. Sometimes the cures had been brought about by yellow serpents sacred to Asclepius, found only within his sanctuary precincts. These, rather strangely, were supposed to have slithered up to the patient in the night and licked the wound which would then miraculously heal.

"I wouldn't want any snake near me if I was ill," came Harry's immediate response when I told him.

"I'd be very willing to be licked by a snake and cured, than not licked and remain in pain," I replied. "I wouldn't mind a snake licking my jaw, or even a tooth if it cured toothache."

"I'd rather go to a Greek dentist, thank you." The remark was followed by an 'oooooof!'

I told Harry about various inscriptions which had been found in the sanctuary, giving details of some of the cures achieved at Epidaurus: a young man, for instance, who'd come with a spear-head lodged in his jaw. A spear-head in his jaw! That really must have been painful! But after a night sleeping in the Abaton, he'd found next day he was holding the spear-head and was completely healed. Another inscription recorded an eyeless man who'd found by morning he had eyes and could see.

The early Christians had, apparently, found the healing powers of the Asclepius sanctuaries, of which Epidaurus was the greatest, a tough nut to crack. They'd declared Asclepius to be an evil demon, who'd taken possession of places on earth because he'd been unable to attain to the purer and more holy region near to the one true God. They'd insisted that it was only Christ who was truly divine and had the proper authority to work miracles.

It was all very mystifying.

It seemed very odd that the relics of a saint had become the source of miracles for Christians. Bones and skulls I found somewhat repulsive. Yet in many Greek Orthodox churches there is often today a valued relic kept in a silver or bejewelled reliquary. I could admire the container but hadn't been conditioned to pore lovingly over skeletal remains.

"Besides," I'd remarked to Harry one day when we'd been discussing the matter, "it's all very well to be the proud possessor of St. George's skull but, if there's another church which also claims to have the skull, then how many skulls can St. George have?" To which Harry had said: "If it performs miracles it doesn't matter."

"But," I'd argued, "only one skull can really be St. George's, which surely means that people can get miracles out of fakes and shams if they have enough faith."

"Absolutely. It all comes from within," came the confident answer. And for once Harry and I had agreed on the matter.

When Christianity took over it must have been far more convenient for people to go to a nearby church to pray and petition, than to travel miles to some far-flung Asclepius sanctuary. If the patient failed to recover in a church, then it was easy for the Christian priest to scratch his head sorrowfully, and say that some lurking unrepented sin had prevented it.

If Christians found this centre of healing at Epidaurus a hard nut to crack, they finally cracked it by example. When, for instance, plague struck, the early Christians excelled by showing themselves compassionate and fearless in the face of danger. It was then that pagans began to think that there must be something in Christianity. To see Christians smiling in adversity; to observe them risking their lives in tending the worst cases of some epidemic; and then to witness them dying with assurance and with the expectation of life - not in Elysium (the Islands of the Blessed), but in a heaven where the greater God, far greater than Zeus, was waiting; and to be told also that Christ, Son of this great God, had burst the bonds of death and Hades could not contain him - all these things must have added up. People wanted miracles and this new Christian faith produced amazing examples of them.

We climbed the stone steps of the Epidaurus theatre, famed throughout the world for its acoustics. It was built up a hillside which was shaped as a natural amphitheatre. Growing through crevices between the tiered seats were pink cyclamen, strangely beautiful against the grey stone.

From our top seats we watched the tour guides go through their routines down below. Reciting Shakespeare, Goethe, Dante, or any other famous national poet, each one went clapping round the circular orchestra (the area where the chorus used to dance) in order to demonstrate how sounds and voices carried upwards from every part of the theatre.

One sylph-like Italian stood alone in the centre of the orchestra on the altar of Dionysos, and gabbled Italian to her group of listeners seated around the lower tiers. We didn't understand her language, but we watched her illustrating the acoustics. She held up a coin and dropped it to the ground, and we heard the tinkle; she struck a match, and we heard it; she shred a piece of paper, and we heard that too.

The Asclepius sanctuaries aimed to heal, not only the afflicted part of the body, but mind and spirit also, hence the temple, stadium, gymnasium and the theatre. The entire Epidaurus complex had been constructed as a therapeutic centre.

Hippocrates, the famous physician of the fifth century B.C., whose early influence is still remembered because of his Hippocratic oath, would have thoroughly approved of this place. He believed in the natural recovery of the body which was made up of a harmony of elements which, when distorted, caused ill health. The pagan Hippocratic oath went: 'I swear by Apollo the physician and Asclepius and Hygiea and Panacea (daughters of Asclepius) invoking all the gods and goddesses to be my witnesses, that I will fulfil this Oath and this written covenant to the best of my power and of my judgment...' In the tenth century, in the oldest Greek manuscript of the Hippocratic text, the above passage was headed by the words: 'from the Oath of Hippocrates according as it may be sworn by a Christian.'

I unscrewed the lid of our water-bottle and surreptitiously swallowed another a pain-killer. I didn't really need it, but wanted to keep any lurking suspect ache at bay.

"You know Hippocrates?" I said to Harry.

"Who?"

"The Hippocratic oath man."

"Oh, him! Is he from here?"

"No. But did you know that when he lived four hundred and something years B.C., he had a theory even then that environment was important to good health? Well, he had. He wrote a treatise on 'Air, Earth and Locality'. I've actually read it, and it's quite contemporary in its views on the environment. Don't you think that rather marvellous, considering he lived all those centuries ago? God knows what he'd think of today's pollution!"

We came down from the theatre and wandered on amongst the ruins, past the baths, the gymnasium, the temple of Asclepius and the round Tholos. Finally, we found ourselves at some outcrop beyond the main excavations, where we walked up a wide ramp which seemed to be a part of something important, but exactly what we couldn't tell. Suddenly from nowhere, or so it seemed - actually from olive and pine trees - a young couple confronted us. A gentle, sweet-faced girl, with shoulder-length dark hair and wearing dark glasses, told us about this ramp. It was, she said, the great Propylaea (the original entrance to the sanctuary), and the end of the Sacred Way for pilgrims coming from the ancient town of Epidaurus by the sea. She apologized for wearing sun-glasses, but said she couldn't take them off because the sun hurt her eyes. She continued to inform us about the site as though she knew it personally.

We thanked her for her information, and then wandered back the way we'd come. We found ourselves once more beside the Tholos, a round ruin about which we knew nothing either. Suddenly the girl and her companion appeared beside us again. The girl now informed us that this was the tomb of Asclepius, the hero. As a deity he had been worshipped in his temple, but as a hero (born of a mortal woman and Apollo) his power had been gathered from the earth. The building was symbolic of a coiled snake which was the sacred symbol of Asclepius, she said.

Our young guide went on to tell us how the Tholos had been a magnificent construction. There had been a round external Doric colonnade supporting a cornice decorated with rosettes. Within had been an inner colonnade, and within that a room with walls of white marble; windows let in the light and there was a floor paved with black and white slabs. The epicentre of this had had a movable stone by which people could gain access to a cellar in which there were three concentric passages, representations yet again of a coiled snake.

At this point she at last removed her sun-glasses to reveal the most beautiful almond-shaped brown eyes. She then informed us that if we wanted to see the finest temples we should go to Sicily. Then, as suddenly as she had come, she was gone again.

"Odd!" I said to Harry.

"What's odd?"

"She sort of vanished."

"Well, she didn't exactly hang around," he agreed.

"She vanished," I insisted. "It was like a visitation from the goddess Athena. She used to appear in disguise to help those she favoured." Harry gave me an odd look.

"You think I'm losing my marbles?" I asked, and waited for reassurance. Instead, Harry said he thought I was which was disconcerting.

For a while I toyed with the thought of being a loony, and watched Harry for signs of anxiety whilst I talked on and tried to be 'normal'.

Quite unexpectedly, he himself suddenly referred to 'the goddess Athena' who had miraculously appeared at our side. "So if she was Athena, who was her companion?" he asked.

"Asclepius?" I suggested.

Since then it has been a story often told to the astonishment of friends and relations, who have eyed us furtively and exchanged glances with each other. Yet somehow in Greece all things are possible, and it is they who are the losers if they look at us askance.

We wandered on away from the ruins, to find somewhere to rest and restore a semblance of sanity to our lives. There were refreshingly cool spots, where visitors could relax under trees and let the site wash over them. We made ourselves comfortable against a pine. The sun shone, keeping up its daily watch over the human creatures who were rambling over this ancient sanctuary made famous by Asclepius.

There'd been other such healing sanctuaries of Asclepius, one of them being on the south side below the Acropolis in Athens which we'd once visited. Under Christianity this had been converted to a large Byzantine church in the fifth or sixth century, and suitably dedicated to the two healing saints, Cosmas and Damian, thus continuing the healing traditions of the place.

I closed my eyes and thought about the mystery of the human body. That on the whole everything worked well together - nerves, muscles, bones and blood, all vacuum-packed in layers of skin, seemed to me nothing less than a miracle; each component part functioned so long as everything else did, otherwise you suffered pain or loss of energy.

A hand groped for mine. "How's the toothache?" But, before I could tell him it had as good as gone, he had jumped up and was brushing himself down, and shaking out his trouser legs. He had been sitting on an ant-hill.

It seems that even the smallest thing can throw the body into disarray and cause discomfort. The marvel, surely, is that there is ever tranquillity and good health, considering the multitude of obstacles to achieving such perfection.

SANCTUARY OF HERA

CHAPTER

3

ARGOS

Harry discovered a map of the Peloponnese in my luggage, and suddenly map-reading became his main preoccupation. A street plan of Naufplion also caught his eye and, after studying it, he made an unexpected announcement.

"Why the hell are we in this alleyway when we could be by the sea?"

"The sea?" I asked. I was so steeped in tracking down old sanctuary sites, that I'd failed to bother with anything else.

"Look at this! There's a bay - boats - ships!"

We left our dreary room, whose ensuite bath-room was in a broom cupboard with a sliding door, went downstairs where the manager of the hotel (disfigured by a large wart on the side of his nose) stood at reception, said 'Kali mera' to him, and walked out into the sunshine. Following the town plan Harry led the way down several narrow side streets, till we came to a wide crescent bay, with the sea a sheen of calm pierced by a stately yacht sailing into harbour. Across the bay on a long promontory a chain of mountains rose from the landmass, and not far away was a small fortified island. Harry consulted his map.

"Bourdzi," he said. "The island of Bourdzi."

The town of Naufplion was built up a hill. We found a hotel higher up with balconies overlooking the bay, and asked if they had a room. We were shown one and booked it at once. Two hours later we had made our getaway from the Wart and the broom cupboard. We felt excessively pleased with ourselves as we sat on our balcony, and stared over mellow russet-coloured roofs to the curve of the harbour, the island of Bourdzi and the distant mountains.

Realizing there was a risk of staying put all day, I voiced my thoughts. "I have to see the Heraion," I said.

The map was inspected again. "Ah, here it is! East of Argos!"

"We can take a bus to Argos and then a taxi," I remarked. "Or we can go to Mycenae today and do the Heraion tomorrow."

Harry was again inspecting the map. "Mycenae. Ah, yes! It's on the Argos road going north-east!"

"There's a bus all the way," I said, slightly suspicious of Harry's new-found occupation.

"What's special about the Heraion? I can see no point in pouring money out on a taxi if - "

"The Heraion is a must," I declared positively.

"Why?"

"It's where the goddess Hera had her temple," I said.

"So? All temple sites are much the same."

"Hera was the wife of Zeus, and it's where the two of them met." Harry was only too ready to dismiss the matter as of no consequence. "Anyway, I'm determined to go to it. If you don't want to you can always stay here," I said firmly.

"No, I'd better come too. You'll only get lost. I'm the one with the map now."

This new authority I could see was going to be a hindrance. I mightn't get lost, but neither might I get where I wanted if Harry took charge of these expeditions and a taxi was involved. As well as the Heraion, I was determined to visit the Agia Moni Convent which was built beside an ancient spring where, it was claimed, the goddess Hera had bathed annually in order to renew her virginity. As I knew Harry wasn't keen to visit nuns, I was prepared to do it alone.

But, for the moment, there seemed to be no great hurry to go anywhere. Instead, Harry sat with his binoculars and watched another yacht sail into harbour.

"Must be coming from - " He consulted the map and saw that ships sailed in from the Saronic Gulf. "It has probably sailed down from Corinth or in from Piraeus," he remarked.

Early that afternoon we caught a bus to Mycenae. But it was the Heraion, the ancient sanctuary site of the goddess Hera which was the jewel for me in the Argolid crown. It was open only in the mornings, and the following day we went to it.

"I need only three minutes," I assured the young man who was unlocking a metal door in the wire mesh perimeter fence surrounding the ancient sanctuary of Hera. At first he had been reluctant to leave his post at the entrance to the Heraion. No, I told him, I did not intend to walk the six or so kilometres to Mycenae, I wanted only to go a little way along this ancient foot-path and then return. "Three minutes only," I repeated.

The young man shrugged as he allowed Harry and me to pass through. He had no understanding whatever why anyone would want to walk briefly on a dirt track; foreigners coming to his country were strange creatures, looking only to the past, with their minds inspired by ancient words and their imaginations spinning into orbit beyond the realities of present day life. I was one of these oddities.

We followed the path flanked by silver-leafed olive trees, then rounded a bend where we saw distant mountains and, in the foreground, the possible ruins of the Mycenaen citadel - well, I liked to think that was what we were looking at. Out came the map, and Harry took his bearings and voiced his doubts. But it hardly mattered if I was wrong, the whole point being that the history and the myths of the place were vivid enough to fill the mind and transport it back three thousand years into antiquity.

The reason for wanting to walk on this particular path was because Agamemnon, King of Mycenae, had once come along it from his palace, and his nobles had sworn their allegiance to him in the presence of the goddess Hera, before setting out for the Trojan War.

"Can you imagine a war being fought because some king's son has seduced another king's wife?" I asked Harry. "Would you go to war for me?"

Harry was evasive. I went on: "Actually, not for me but because my sister had run off with another man?"

"Is that what happened?" He still had that evasive look.

"Well, you've heard of Helen of Troy?"

"Yes, Helen, of course!"

"Who actually wasn't of Troy at all but was from the Peloponnese and married to King Menelaus of Sparta, Agamemnon's brother."

"And I've heard of Sparta."

"Have you heard of the Judgement of Paris?"

"I've heard of it - but - " He made a vague gesture hoping for enlightenment.

"Well - " And I told him how the war had been triggered, even planned, by Strife who'd thrown a golden apple down at the wedding of some noble with the words 'for the fairest' written on it. It was given to Paris, son of the King of Troy, to present to whoever he thought the most beautiful of the three goddesses: Hera, Athena or Aphrodite. They each promised him a reward. Hera promised him land, Athena wisdom, and Aphrodite the most beautiful woman in the world. He dismissed the first boring prizes and chose the most beautiful woman. Whereupon matters were so arranged that he came to Sparta, was entertained by Helen and fell hopelessly in love with her.

"To confuse matters more Helen was also the sister of Clytemnestra, Agamemnon's wife," I told Harry. "Honour had to be satisfied so war was inevitable. They came here to the Heraion to get Hera's blessing as she was goddess and protectress of marriage."

We had already allowed the three minutes to stretch to five, or even longer, and began to retrace our steps. The young man was waiting, and mildly admonished us with a glance at his watch. Once back inside the perimeter fence he closed and locked the metal gate behind us, and we were left alone to explore the ancient Heraion.

I was enchanted with the place. Built on three terraces there had been three successive temples, each replacing the former when it had been destroyed by fire. The view from the terraces was panoramic and took in the wide sweep of the Argolid plain with its back-cloth of mountains, and the sea like the brim of a hat at the horizon.

"The sea is south-west," Harry remarked as he sat on a rock with his map open on his lap.

"'Scuse me, you look now to Argos?" A lone woman, who turned out to be Swedish, stood pleasantly beside us, obviously hoping to strike up our acquaintance. "You say that it is Argos?"

"Yes," I agreed.

"And is that then Mycenae?"

"No."

"It is not the Mycenae? Ah." She herself opened her guide-book and examined the possibilities. "Yes, I am wrong - wrong! Here, it is named the Larissa acropolis!" The woman was in her forties, with long fair hair tied in a pony tail, and glistening hair on her upper lip; slight freckles covered her nose and forehead. I noticed she had a wedding-ring.

"You are alone?" I enquired.

"Yes. I am free! Quite free! It is so goooood!" she exclaimed, flinging her arms up to the sky in exultation. "Five years I have separated from my husband, the bastard! And then I have such a man - at first he is a god! He too is the bloody bastard! What pain I have! A minute, please!" And she took our binoculars, raised them to her eyes and looked at the sea, then trained them round the mountains. "It is so good! This, it is so goooood!"

In the plain the town of Argos was a clutter of houses. "Please - I stop you!" She handed back the binoculars but stood beside me restlessly, with a hand ready to take them back. I couldn't ignore the hand and soon she had them again. "Look at that! Look at that! Wow!"

On the Larissa acropolis at a considerable height, there had once been an ancient shrine of Hera Akraia (Hera of the Summit) which, in the Christian era, had been replaced by a church, the 'Panagia tou Vrachou' (the 'Virgin of the Rock').

"You are a professor?" asked the Swede adjusting the lens of the binoculars.

"Not at all."

"I am glad. My husband he was professor and a bastard! I hate all professors! There, you take them now. The boy-friend I have afterwards, he is army and oh, he too is the bastard! But now I am so free! I am happy after so many years pain! You understand me?"

"Your English is very good," I said politely.

"Thank you."

She followed me around from terrace to terrace. There was no site-plan, and it was difficult to piece together the ruins and create some vision of splendour which, undoubtedly, the site had once presented with its columned temples. The Swedish woman told me she was an architect and pointed out the drainage system where there had been ancient baths used for purification, and the annual Heraion festival and games. I told her that I'd read that at one time there'd been in Hera's temple a great cult statue made of gold and ivory. In one hand she had held a sceptre and in the other a pomegranate, which in her case was a symbol of fruitfulness and fertility. These attributes had spilled over into Christian art. And I went on to tell her how the British scholar, Marina Warner, in her book Alone of All Her Sex, had written about a Christian equivalent at Paestum, not far from Naples, where a statue, known as the Madonna of the Pomegranate, resembled the ancient one of Hera here at the Heraion. Apparently, the Madonna had held a pomegranate in one hand, and in the other a staff with a cuckoo on top. Marina Warner had pointed out how the cuckoo was the harbinger of spring, and how Hera in that respect had presided over the season of new life, which in Christianity began on March 25, the spring equinox, and the feast of the Annunciation.

" 'Scuse me, Annunciation, what is it?"

"Oh, sorry. It's when the Angel Gabriel came to the Virgin Mary and announced she was to have a son."

"Ah. It is March 25th?"

"Yes. Though I didn't know that until I read Marina Warner's book."

I had never particularly wondered what the word meant, it was just a day in the Church calendar. Even when I'd begun to look into the matter, it had been a long time before I made the connection and had realized that the 25th December (the birth of Christ) was exactly nine months later. In fact, Christ's date of birth had never been mentioned in the Gospels; it was only finally fixed several hundred years into the Christian era.

"But, of course, it is not true! They are fairy stories all these things. You are not believing in Christianity?"

I looked at her. I might be a sceptic, but I was in no way prepared to go along with her apparent atheism. But her mind was already back on the Heraion.

"It is here that the god first sees his goddess," she went on.

The story of Zeus setting eyes on Hera for the first time explained the symbolic cuckoo. Behind the Heraion rose the Mt. Euboea massif, otherwise known as Cuckoo Mountain. According to legend, when Zeus first set eyes on Hera, he fell instantly in love with her, and came down to her in the form of a bedraggled cuckoo. Hera took the poor, distressed creature on her lap, whereupon Zeus turned into the god he was and ravished her. They married and their honeymoon lasted for three hundred years.

"He is the bastard this god! His poor wife! She is so unhappy! So jealous! Always Zeus he is in love with another woman!"

"I like the stories of the old pagan gods," I admitted.

"You like them?"

"I can understand them. They are very human."

I sat down on the base of a column, with strangely haunting thoughts about the old Olympian gods. How real they had been to those who'd lived those three thousand years ago. Christians would say they did not exist except as poetic figments of the imagination. Yet, under these so-called figments, men had excelled. The pagan gods were just as real to men then, as God is to those who believe today. One reason, perhaps, why I liked them was that they had never threatened with hell and damnation or demanded worship as had the Jewish God. In pagan times, men had honoured and had sacrificed to the gods, hoping in return for their divine protection. If marriage had been a matter for concern, men would honour Hera; if justice, then Athena; if abundance of crops, then Demeter, and so on.

It was its isolation and proximity to nature which made the Heraion exceptional. Only one other couple wandered about amongst the ancient columns, and I wished Hilda would attach herself to them. But, instead, she clambered about from boulder to boulder, column to column, as she followed after me. A slight haze hung over the panoramic view, and a light breeze was pleasantly cooling in the midday sun. A few fluffy white clouds sailed in the sky like cottonwool puffs in an eternity of blue.

Hera's jealousy and petulance against the extra-marital affairs of her dear husband were understandable, especially as she herself remained faithful to him. Despite their three hundred years honeymoon, however, she produced only two sons, the seldom heard of Ares, god of war, and Hephaestus, who was a cripple. Some say he became crippled because Hera flung him from her on Mt. Olympus, others that he was born with the soles of his feet back to front so that he walked in an odd manner. He was, however, a wonderfully gifted and skilled craftsman. He could fashion anything in gold and silver. It was he who built the gold palaces of the gods on Mt. Olympus.

"You have visited Nemea?" enquired Hilda.

"No."

"I like to go but I cannot, I have no car. You have car?"

"No."

"How you come. You walk?"

"No. We came by taxi."

I was getting her drift. Why was it that so many lone women regarded themselves as prodigies of resourceful womanhood, and of particular interest to others who might cross their path. I found their proud independence irritating because it inevitably trespassed on my privacy. Feminine wiles were never far away.

"You have a taxi back to Argos?"

"Yes."

"Ah, so. It is O.K. I come with you? If no, I can walk. I am strong and have time. I like to walk."

I tried to smile, whilst thinking 'oh, hell!' and said that it would be fine.

"It is not a problem?"

"It's not a problem." I looked at my watch and saw that there were another twenty minutes before the taxi.

"I like I visit Nemea. They tell me it is very interesting and it is not far. It is where Hercules he kills the lion. I forget how it is Hercules he kills the lion, I know only that his father he is Zeus, and his mother is a woman who is not his wife - the bastard!" She stooped down to pick a wild flower which she carefully placed between the pages of her guide-book, arranging its leaves and petals for pressing. "I like always to take with me a flower to remind me where I have been," she explained. She put the guide-book back in a small knapsack, then stood up.

"And you know the story of the giant they call Argus?" she went on. "It happens here at Argos. He is the one with a hundred eyes sent to guard the beautiful Io. Io, she is a priestess here at Hera's temple. And Zeus - he is so much the bastard! - he falls in love with Io and he turns her into a small cow."

"Heifer," I corrected.

"You are right. She is the heifer. But Hera, she knows of this new love, and she sends Argus the giant with the hundred eyes to guard Io from Zeus. Then Zeus, he asks his son Hermes - oh, he is so much the bastard! - Hermes, he also is the son of Zeus from another woman! He asks his son Hermes to kill this giant with his hundred eyes. And this is difficult because he can see all ways. But Hermes has a plan. He plays on the Pan-pipes and it is a lullaby so all the eyes of Argus they close for him to sleep. And when he sleeps Hermes he kills him. They say it is how the peacock gets the beautiful tail, because Hera puts in the tail of the peacock all the eyes of Argus. You know this story?"

"I only remember that Hera set a gadfly on poor Io the

heifer, and it so tormented her that she went all over the world trying to get away from it."

"I think Hera is not kind. But when you are unhappy - when your husband he is a bastard - you are then cruel."

Harry came up and joined us. Hilda was ecstatic because he had a map, and asked to be shown exactly where we were, where Nemea was, where Lerna was. I eyed her watchfully as she pored over the map, her head unnecessarily bent close to Harry's who, true to his suspicion of foreigners was drawing away the more hers got closer.

"Your wife - you are his wife?" she raised her head to look at me.

"Yes."

"She says to me I can come with you in the taxi to Argos? Is this O.K.? I can walk, of course."

She asked us where we were staying. I gave Harry a sharp prod which seemed to make him cough out the name of our hotel before he could stop it.

"But that is so nice! Naufplion! I too stay at Naufplion! Perhaps tonight we meet and we eat at a taverna?"

"What a pity," I said, "we have a Greek family we are visiting tonight."

"Tomorrow?"

"We leave tomorrow."

"Ah, that is so sad. I must eat alone. Just as I meet you, I must say good-bye. And I like you. I see you are good - you are not the bastard!"

When our taxi came, our Swede's whole demeanour sparkled with renewed excitement. The driver was in his thirties, and the proud possessor of a brand new Mercedes. He had only had his taxi for four days, he told us, and was eager to go anywhere, do anything. "Nemea? Yes, yes! Of course, I know!"

We got out at Argos and watched as our Swede got into the front seat beside him. The opportunities which lay ahead for her were numerous, and the Mercedes and its driver a decided shot in the arm. She had already learned he was unmarried, and that his parents ran an estate with orange and lemon groves. Would she learn that he too might be a bastard? Or would he learn that she was one?

The following morning Kostas, our hotel proprietor, said he would drive me to Agia Moni as he had matters to attend to nearby. I was delighted as it was a good opportunity for Greek conversation aided by his excellent knowledge of English.

We drove out on the Epidaurus road, then turned right into the hills. Soon we came to a tall whitewashed building with a row of windows along its highest level. Kostas told me he would return in thirty minutes.

I found the entrance, and came first to a small chapel down several steps. On the far wall inside the building was a glistening mosaic of the Virgin Mary seated on a chalice from either side of which water gushed. I supposed this was the site of the holy spring but there was nobody around to ask.

I walked on to the main monastery complex where there were orange trees and flower-beds, with the occasional cypress standing sentinel. A tiny nun greeted me outside a small domed Byzantine church. She had a gaunt, almost skull-like face with large, gentle, luminous brown eyes. I asked her if I might look inside, and she inclined her head in a gesture of assent. A priest and a nun were coming from a side door of the sanctuary; their morning service must have just ended.

The Byzantine church itself was exquisite with its frescoed barrel-roofed ceiling and dome. Could I take photos, I enquired? Again the gesture of the head indicated that I could. In the narthex there was a fresco - the only one I'd ever seen - of God seated on a cloud with various words of wisdom written above and below, whose translation ran something like: 'on one side good, the other side with the fear of God - Speak well, speak in the fear of God'. God looked benign and kindly, and I wondered why the word 'fear' was necessary.

To one side of the door there was a large icon of the Virgin Mary; she was again seated on a chalice with the Christ child on her lap, and the fountain of life gushing either side of the chalice into a round basin below. Lower still on this icon lay a man with one arm up beseechingly, and a small black devil springing from his mouth, whilst the water of life trickled from the bowl down to him. Near him was another figure having the water of life poured down his throat. And, on the right, a man was tending a living plant as he looked on anxiously at the resuscitation of the two sinners.

All these were poetic images to impress the mind with spiritually uplifting messages. It really didn't matter if one believed or not, in fact it didn't really matter if it was true or not. What mattered was the elevation of the mind from 'Oh, the bastard!' to 'What can I do to help him?' thoughts. Nothing can be unbelievable once the mind has given an idea shape and form and, therefore, life. From life blossoms hope.

Whilst the tiny nun accompanied me on a tour, she told me she had been there sixty years and was now aged eighty. She took me to the monastery workshop where there were several looms; all the work for sale there had been woven or stitched or crocheted by the nuns, she said. I bought a table-cloth and a history of the monastery, and asked my guide to sign her name in it. She wrote Elisabet, and then asked me my name. She could not pronounce it, and I wrote it in Greek the way I knew it should be spelt: Tzil. She assured me she would pray for me - a misunderstanding, perhaps, as I hadn't asked her to - but I wasn't averse to having a prayer said on my behalf.

As I was about to leave, I suddenly remembered that the whole purpose of my visit was to see the holy spring where Hera had bathed annually to renew her virginity. I found another nun and enquired whether the small chapel, with the mosaics portraying the Virgin Mary as the holy source of life, marked the site of the ancient spring? She told me to come with her, then indicated I should follow three members of a family making their way round to the lower outer wall of the convent.

So this was it! An arched recess of stonework in a whitewashed wall. In the recess were a number of marble plaques carved with emblems. Below these was a waterspout, out of which the spring flowed into a short gulley and poured down into a large wide bowl to overflow sideways through a pipe into a fish-pond below. Each member of the family was filling a vessel with the water to take away; one woman cupped her hands and drank the water. When they left, I walked down the steps and let the water run over my fingers. The marble plaques in the recess were of Christian emblems, but one of them was of peacock feathers; I was reminded at once of the goddess Hera because of the legend in which she had set the numerous eyes of the giant, Argus, killed by Hermes, in a peacock's tail.

In the book about the history of the monastery I became curious as to why it was called in Greek 'Agia Moni Areias'. The printed words suggested that it was genitive, in other words 'of Areia'. Had the 'H' been dropped? Could it have been an overlap from pagan times to Christianity and have been a spelling variation of Hera's name?

I took one last look at this holy spring before I turned reluctantly away. It was interesting that it was as much the spring of life identified with the Virgin Mary now, as once it had been the holy spring of the goddess Hera.

Kostas was waiting and seemed ready to continue my Greek conversation. I asked him about family life in Greece, and the influence of the Church on morality. He said that there was very little crime, and he thought the Orthodox Church and the family link to it due to the feast-days of saints and, therefore, the name days of individuals, had a bearing on this.

I began to tell him my views on the Church of England, how I believed it had lost its grip on people in its efforts to appear understanding and forgiving. So understanding had it become that nothing was particularly sinful any longer. In fact, it had become so fragmented in its views that few people took it very seriously nowadays. To put it bluntly, I thought that matters had become so confused that there should be a new service for the unbaptising of people. That way we could all start again.

Kostas nodded. In fact he seemed to agree with everything I said, and I began to suspect he wasn't listening at all, which was possibly just as well. He had, I knew, got problems of his own which he was probably mulling over. One of the waitresses at the hotel had become totally impossible. She was middle-aged and bolshy and wore shorts. She clearly had a heap of personal difficulties which she confided loudly to others in the dining-room as she plonked plates and cutlery before the startled guests. Harry and I had nicknamed her Pursed Lips.

Whatever Kostas' thoughts were, I returned to the hotel in time for breakfast, and Harry and I had another bout of Pursed Lips serving us in a rage.

Harry's new found devotion to map-reading continued to fill his time. Any place I mentioned brought out the map. Nestor's Palace? Yes, there it was north of Pylos! Andritsina - where? Ah, there in the mountains! And Olympia? Yes, it was north-west of Andritsina! The map itself was becoming worn, and a hole was appearing in its folds.

Before leaving Naufplion we visited the great Palamidhi Venetian fortress behind the town. It was an extraordinary feat of human capability. Its massively thick stone walls with arrow slits in them, or the wider ones for muskets, were trained on all the approaches by land or sea. Brick-built beehive type look-out posts crowned the highest points of the walls. Harry was in his element with map and compass, pointing out the lines of approach the enemy might make, sailing in from the Saronic Gulf or the Aegean Sea; or marching overland from north or west - or south or east, for that matter.

"Is that Argos across the bay there?" I asked.

Map consultation. "Must be," Harry agreed.

"In that case there is the Heraion," I said excitedly. "And over there must be Mycenae."

"And if you look eastwards you might pick out your

convent," Harry remarked, turning with the binoculars to his eyes. Suddenly he seized my elbow and hissed into my ear not to look. He began hurrying me away. All the arrow slits in the world could not defend us when the danger lay within the fortress walls. It was the Swedish woman. And with her wearing dark glasses was the well-heeled taxi driver. We were gone before they spotted us.

4

CORFU - DODONA

We landed in Corfu in the early hours when it was still dark, though a faint light streaked the horizon. We asked a taxi driver to take us to a 'B' class pension if he knew of one, preferably near the ferry-boats. I was thinking of the convenience of taking a ferry on to the mainland which was the whole purpose of this trip.

We drove at speed into the dawn, and soon were in the dock area and heading for a beautiful white cruise liner newly docked from Brindisi. Our driver called out to an elderly woman in carpet slippers who was waddling forward to the quayside on the watch for disembarking passengers wanting accommodation. We, however, were to be her morning's catch, and her brown face was wreathed in a plump smile as she took our hands and led the way to her small pension close by.

Asking many questions as is the habit with Greeks - where were we from, and where were we going, and what did our family consist of - she took us upstairs to a dark landing. There she showed us a small and rather sordid room with its own squalid bath-room, and ran the taps to demonstrate the plumbing worked.

We were too tired, or too polite, to say no to it. Worse still we were asked to pay in advance, and I paid her for two nights. She was so pleased with the money, or perhaps my attempts to speak Greek, that she seized my head between her two plump hands and planted a fat kiss on both cheeks.

We stretched out on our un-ironed grey-white sheets, and stared at the dirty pastel-coloured walls and gimcrack furniture held together with blobs of glue. From where I lay, propped against some beastly bolster of a pillow (stuffed with dead rats from the feel of it), I could see where the window frame didn't fit and there were chinks of light between window and wall. The view from it was of the dirty cement-rendered adjoining building.

"How sordid can we get?" I remarked.

"And you've paid for two nights! It's bad enough paying for one, but for two!"

"I'm sorry. You saw the woman - she simply took us over and got the money from me before I had time to think. You weren't much help, may I say!"

"Well, we've paid for it now so we can't get out of it. Bad luck!" And he turned over and put his hands under his head to keep it from contact with the pillow.

As a sop to taking two weeks instead of one, as Harry had wanted, I'd promised him several days on Corfu doing nothing. Well, not quite nothing but erring on the side of idleness.

Later that morning as part of our 'idleness' we explored the old town of Kerkyra where I found the Church of Agios Spiridion. St. Spiridion is the patron saint of Corfu, and is held in great esteem by the Corfiots as in the past he'd repelled Turkish invasion, cured the islanders of the plague, and had performed many miracles of healing.

As we wandered about the church looking at its icons and frescoes, a party of Greek women was suddenly summoned to see the saint himself lying in a side chapel. I asked a woman if I could join them and, with the customary little nod and gesture of the hand to stand beside her, I left Harry and advanced with the women towards the candle-lit scene.

Two priests were officiating, one at the head and one at the foot of the saint. As we inched closer the women began to cross themselves. I asked an elderly one beside me what the procedure was. She told me I should kiss the saint's feet, move along the body and then kiss the glass over his face. Not being used to such devotions I said I didn't want to kiss him. The woman looked startled, and I tried to explain that I wished to see but, being English and all that, I wasn't used to kissing saints. She accepted this quietly as we slowly advanced.

I became absurdly apprehensive as we drew closer. I could now see that one of the priests had a fistful of scraps of paper. He was, I suspected, praying for the sick or the souls of the departed whose names he had been given. One woman who had already been up stood looking back towards the scene, crossing herself repeatedly as though wound up and unable to stop. Her lips moved in prayer, and the word 'Spiridion' was recognisably mouthed many times.

We were now up the steps and in the candle-lit area. I felt the priest's eyes on me as I solemnly bowed my head over a pair of red and silver brocade slippered feet. I was affected by the sanctity of the scene, whilst also feeling it was lunacy on my part performing these reverential acts.

I followed the woman in front of me along the length of the body which was covered with red fabric adorned with ribbons and other bits and pieces, some of which looked much like ribbons of tinfoil. I reached the head of the saint, and the priest prayed as I dutifully bowed.

What I saw startled me. I'd been expecting a peacefully embalmed face and, instead, I saw a dark wizened one turned sideways to the torso grinning at me. I moved away quickly, and made my way through the many women looking back and crossing themselves and whispering prayers. I was thoroughly unnerved. Was it possible that where I'd seen ugliness others had seen beauty?

I returned to the dark recesses at the back where Harry was waiting for me. "So how was St. Thingummy?" he asked in a whisper, loud enough to be heard by everyone. I mumbled something like 'very nice', then muttered: "Not in here. Come outside."

We went out into the glaring sunlight and I was glad to be amongst the living; to join the strolling, ice-cream-licking tourists. I caught a snatch of English gossip: "She's a bit too involved, you know what I mean? And how did you get on with Nikos?" What did any of them care about death and saints? It was life - LIFE! that they were on the island for. LIFE was being played out all around us and it was time to take part in it.

Before coming on this trip I'd read Lawrence Durrell's book Prospero's Cell in which he wrote about his time on Corfu as a young man. I learned there were few sanctuary sites on Corfu, but he wrote that at Kassiopi, a small fishing village in the north-east of the island, there had once been a temple of Zeus, believed to have been where the church now stood.

We joined the mass of jostling tourists in their shorts, sandals and sun-hats, and caught a bus to Kassiopi. Soon we were on our way, passing the many hoardings announcing such tourist delights as 'Boat trips with Captain Homer', 'Angela's sexy girls', 'Live B.B.C. TV', 'British pub food', 'Real ale and fish and chips', and so on. These pronouncements reassured Harry that British food was available, and he wouldn't have to face 'turópitta', or 'kalamarákia' or other suspect foreign dishes.

We left the outskirts of Kerkyra and followed the coast road, passing terraced olive groves. Way below was the sea with inlets and small coves fringed with cypresses. Large cacti grew by the roadside, and every now and then, when the bus stopped at remote country areas, whiffs of hot rosemary and sun-drenched pine-needles flooded in.

Arriving at Kassiopi we were put down in the central plateia, and I asked a stall holder for the church. I was pointed down a path which eventually led to it. Harry assumed we were heading for the sea, which we were, but arrived first at the small whitewashed building in its own courtyard with oleanders growing against the railings.

"A church!" I feigned surprise, though I doubt Harry was taken in.

If this was the old temple site, then worshippers arriving there by boat or down the mountain tracks, would have seen it nestling there several hundred metres inland. It was here that the Emperor Nero, who had fancied himself as a singer and dancer (nobody had dared put him wise as to his lack of talent), had come to sing and dance within the temple precincts. I rather liked the picture of this emperor cavorting in and out between the columns.

"So where's the sea?" Harry was suspicious.

"Oh, the sea! Yes, of course!"

We left the church which was surrounded by supermarkets, holiday accommodation and all the other paraphernalia of modern tourism, and followed a cliff path. We passed many bodies lying on small sandy inlets, or basking on rocks, until we found our own private rocky inlet. Here the sea sparkled and lapped lazily.

Swimming was for me something of a penance as I always felt I was drowning rather than swimming. But it was a salve for saints. I crept down the razor sharp rocks and submerged myself in the cool Ionian waters. Soon Harry was in too and doing the breast-stroke towards Albania, before basking with his toes turned up to the sun.

So the time passed with reading, swimming and 'idling'. The sun was low when the bus took us back to Kerkyra; we seemed to be driving into a black wall of olive groves. Looking back the way we'd come, the olive groves were shadowed and silvery, with glinting telegraph wires looped above them. We were passing bays where caiques and sailing boats were moored. The sea was inky black, smooth as oil. Yes, Corfu was beautiful.

That evening we had dinner at a hotel not far from our pension. The thought of spending our first two nights in our squalid room seemed an affront to the finer things in life. On my second glass of wine I announced: "I can't bear the thought of going back to that disgusting room of ours."

"Well, you've done it now - too late to change your mind now you've paid for it," said the would-be controller of our money. "Two nights! To think you paid for two nights!"

"Bed bugs!" I murmured.

"Bed bugs?" Harry's eyes shot wide open.

He continued to eat in silence for a while, then said: "No, we'll just have to grin and bear it."

"You think so?" I could see 'bed bugs' were having the desired effect.

"I don't think we have to grin and bear anything," I remarked. "Our first two nights and that's the best we can do for ourselves?" I queried. "We don't want to fall ill before we've even started."

"Hum."

"Suppose I ask the price of rooms here? There's no harm in just asking." And, with a parting murmur in his ear of 'bed bugs', I went to the reception desk, was told the price (very reasonable), and from there was taken up to a room large enough to swing twenty cats instead of the half cat of a room we'd paid for. I promptly booked it and returned to Harry in the highest spirits. By now he had considered bugs and hygiene for long enough to want to move.

After supper, we returned to what from then on we regarded as our 'lock-up garage', seized the necessary things for the night, and crept away into the dark with excuses ready of having met friends in Kerkyra.

We woke next morning and basked on the bed, propped up against snow-white, feather pillows. We were able to gaze at the bay, part of which was visible past the jutting corner of our hotel. There were ships at anchor and, beyond them, an outcrop of rocks fringed by pine trees, behind which was the hazy outline of mountains.

"So come on, how was St. Thingummy?" Harry asked

from the depths of his pillows.

"What? You want me to tell you while we're still on his island?"

Harry regarded me critically. "You don't want to let these saints get to you, you know," he said.

But I was not to be drawn.

The following day we took a ferry-boat from Corfu to Igoumenitsa, a small port on the Greek mainland. As we sailed from Kerkyra, we watched the receding shore-line with the old town stacked up behind the port.

We sat on deck beside a family of peasants and began to talk. Soon we learned that they too were travelling on by bus from Igoumenitsa to Ioannina, the capital of the province of Epirus, an important university town made famous during Turkish domination by the tyrant Ali Pasha.

As we were about to disembark, our travelling companions told us to keep with them. The elderly husband led the way with both arms weighed down by two heavy suit-cases. He never looked around but seemed confident that his wife was somewhere behind, with us at her heels. He led us from the docks through the crowded streets to the bus station.

Our bus took us through the mountains, through a wooded area of plane trees whose leaves exuded the powerful aroma of incense. Then we were above the tree-line, and only the odd blasted oak was to be seen on the barren mountainside. Far below we could see the occasional village.

Our driver was a dashing young Greek who seemed

to think he could drive safely without the usual religious talismans. Instead, he had a pair of female lips stuck to his mirror and several long-lashed female eyes. His lack of religious faith somewhat disturbed me until I noticed a small medallion of the Virgin and Child dangling near his steering-wheel.

"So come on, how was St. Thingummybob?" Harry asked again.

"What? You want me to tell you while we're driving through the mountains?" Once more I was not to be drawn. I feared for our safety and wouldn't have been surprised had I seen the saint flying alongside the bus, and grinning at me through the window. Such was my superstitious fear of the unaccountable. Or, perhaps, it was an inner knowledge that there were powers beyond my comprehension, and it was as well to honour them.

We arrived at Ioannina in the afternoon. There we found a small hotel between the bus station and Lake Pambotis (where Ali Pasha used to drown the women of his harem when they fell from favour). From our bedroom we could hear the revolting sound of somebody trying to clear his throat downstairs. However, our room was clean, and to have arrived at all was exciting. At last the real purpose of this trip was beginning. The following day I planned to visit the famous oracle of Zeus at Dodona.

We were high in the Pindos mountains when our taxi driver pulled up abruptly in a lay-by and told us to get out. It crossed my mind he planned to shoot us, and I clung rather stupidly to my bag. But no, he was no brigand; he was genuinely friendly and eager for us to take a look at the spectacular view of Ioannina far below beside Lake Pambotis which lay still and mysterious, its reflections of Ioannina like a Canaletto masterpiece.

Soon we were winding down from the mountains to a wide plateau. The whole lndscape was enclosed within the surrounding hills and mountains.

"Why are we coming here?" Harry enquired, showing sudden interest.

"Because of the great oracle of Zeus."

"Oh, him, yes. What did he oraculate about?"

"Anything - everything. People with knotty problems would come for guidance. The rustling leaves of his sacred oak tree gave the answer to their questions."

"That sounds unlikely."

"Well, that's what they did," I replied. "Nobody would have bothered with this place if they hadn't known from experience it was worth the effort."

"Ummm!"

"You can't dismiss it," I said defensively. "At the time it was taken very seriously. Rulers sent envoys with questions regarding matters of state: whether to go to war or not; to colonize or not to colonize; to marry or not to marry. All sorts of questions were put to the tree. It's no more odd than people today reading their horoscopes, consulting clairvoyants, or taking on trust what a gypsy sees in the palm of a hand or in a crystal ball."

"But we don't consult the Almighty or expect him to answer a question by sending signs in a yew tree in the churchyard," Harry remarked.

"Only because we haven't been conditioned to thinking like that. The Church reads all sorts of things into a wooden cross, if you look at it that way."

We found a seat and sat down to study the site-plan. In

a booklet on Dodona there was a photograph of its theatre before and after excavation. It was astonishing what work had been undertaken to uncover the many tiers of seats. It was even more surprising that in ancient times people had made their way to this remote area connected to Thessaly by the Metsovian pass cutting through the Pindos mountains - or from any other direction, for that matter - to consult the god, or to watch a drama.

From the rustling of the leaves of the sacred oak tree the priestesses would interpret the god's answers. Zeus, it was believed, dwelt in the roots of his oak, and his power rose to the leaves.

The whole area had a quality about it of peace and solitude, and of a divine energy to which mundane humans could plug in in order to receive strength and guidance. As we pored over the plan I noticed the perpetual rustling of leaves in the nearby trees. It seemed that the wind was funnelled towards us between two distant lofty mountains, and so the leaves were in perpetual motion.

Time seemed of no consequence whilst sitting there. I had the feeling that we were alone under the wide expanse of sky, yet securely contained on all sides by the landscape of mountains; suspended in eternity, as though held to the world in a hammock slung from the heavens.

It is interesting that Olympias (mother of Alexander the Great) came from Dodona, and her family claimed to be descended from Achilles (of Achilles heel fame). As for Alexander, his lineage through the Macedonian kings, was believed to come from Lord Zeus himself. No wonder Alexander thought, or at least encouraged the thought in others, that he was a son of a god, even Dionysos incarnate (Dionysos, son of Zeus), thus promoting belief in his invincibility. His mother had been a devout follower of

Dionysos.

The Dodona oracle was mentioned by Homer in The Iliad. During the Trojan War, Achilles had been nursing a grievance against King Agamemnon because the king had stolen his beautiful slave girl who should have been his by rights. Regarding it as a personal insult, Achilles had laid down his arms and had refused to fight. However, when Agamemnon and his army had been on the point of defeat, Achilles' close companion, Patroclus, had joined the battle. Achilles had prayed to Zeus: '"Zeus, king, lord of Dodona..."' and he'd beseeched him to protect his friend and bring him safely back. The gods, however, were unable to interfere in the life and death of mortals. This rested with the Fates (the Moirai). The modern word in Greek for 'fate' is 'moira'. It was believed that one of the Fates assigned man's lot at birth, the second spun the thread of life and the third cut it at the end of the allotted life span. So Zeus was able to grant the first part of Achilles' prayer by strengthening the heart of his friend, but he wasn't able to prevent his death in battle which depended on the Fate who cut the thread of life.

From the village about half a mile away came the tinkle of sheep bells. A cock began to crow repeatedly, then a donkey brayed as though it had a message of doom which was strangling it. I thought how odd it was that there existed a multitude of languages which humans spoke depending where they lived, whereas animals made their own familiar sound whatever country they were in - a donkey brayed and a cock crowed wherever it was. Besides, humans tended to interpret what was said according to their own perceptions, which often led to considerable error. They had a great capacity to alter speech or written words to suit their own ambitions, whims or hopes.

I began to mull over prophecies. I vacillated hopelessly between Christianity's belief in the fulfilment of Old Testament prophecy, and the questioning of oracles by pagans about existing personal problems.

"It's all very odd," I remarked.

"What is?"

"The Old Testament prophets predicting Christ's birth centuries ahead."

"What's odd about that?"

"Surely people are only interested in the immediate future, in something that might occur during their lifetime?"

"I shouldn't let it bother you."

"I'm only bothered because one's supposed to believe what's written. And what's written can be interpreted in so many ways by different groups - Jews, Christians, Moslems - "

Harry began folding up the site-plan. "Well, I predict it's going to rain," he said.

Turning to look along the wide sweep of plateau, I saw a black cloud masking a far mountain peak. There was nothing like the evidence of one's own eyes to glean the future.

I continued to ponder the phenomenon of prophecies. Isaiah's words: 'Behold a virgin shall be with child, and shall bring forth a son', are ingrained in Christian minds, repeated annually at school Nativity plays, and in churches, as proof of God's plan to send his Son into the world. It is taken from St. Matthew 1:23 which quotes from the Greek translation of Isaiah 7:14. Where the original Hebrew word was 'almah', meaning 'young girl of marriageable age', the Greek translation of 'almah' was 'parthenos' (virgin).

In fact, in those pre-Christian centuries, it was not so

unusual for those of exceptional ability and charisma to be believed to have been immaculately conceived. Pythagoras and Plato were two of them, and Alexander the Great another.

It was worth noting that the oracle of Apollo at Delphi, and the even older one at Dodona, were both functioning in their own strange ways before the hebrew prophets, and centuries before Isaiah who began to prophesy around 740 B.C.

We heard a rumble of thunder in the distance. I remembered that in antiquity thunder in a clear sky meant good fortune. I felt Zeus was watching over us - this supreme and ancient deity had his eye on the two mortals who had come so far to see his sanctuary.

We began to wander, and found the ruined outline of the temple of Zeus himself. There were many young oak trees growing within its precincts, and I wondered if they were the offspring of the original. The famous ancient one had been uprooted by the Christians - uprooted and exposed for what it was, an oak tree with roots!

We continued to explore the sanctuary; we had the place to ourselves except for one other couple. With the help of our site-plan we discovered a temple of Themis, mother of the Fates, and the temple of Hercules where a very early Christian basilica had been built only to be destroyed by earthquake; its cruciform outline could still be seen. I found it odd that so many early basilicas had been destroyed in this way, and thought how the ancient gods must have conspired together to make life uneasy for the Christians. If the pagan gods had been anything at all, and clearly people thought they had been, then why should they succumb to Christianity without a murmur? I could imagine their objections: "By Jove! by gum! these mortals are all suddenly declaring we are evil demons! How dare they turn their backs on us like that. An earthquake! Let us send an earthquake and crash their basilicas to the ground!" And that is what happened - the earthquakes, I mean.

The cloud over the far mountain peak was darkening, and other clouds were piling up around. The occasional rumble of thunder was becoming more frequent, and we began to fear the impending storm. The clouds were massively dense and dark, tossed high to the heavens and lined with gleaming silver.

As we waited for the next bus to take us back to Ioannina, we were offered a lift by the couple we had seen wandering around. Almost at once it began to rain. Large torrential drops battered the roof and deluged against the windscreen. For the duration of the storm we remained stationary, cocooned together in the car.

They had to raise their voices in order to be heard above the drumming of the rain. We learned the couple came from Holland. The man was a biochemist who had just attended a conference in Salonika, and they were now taking a holiday.

Forked lightning zipped down from the sky, and a moment later there was an almighty clap of thunder, and the woman gave a cry of 'aaaaah!' and put her arms over her head.

Her husband ignored the spectacle of his wife cowering and, speaking perfect English, told us how she was a keen archaeologist. "My wife is very interested in Dodona and in all ancient sites. She likes the way that in those times the gods guided the minds of men by forewarning or encouraging them with good or bad omens. Isn't that right, Griet?" The woman put her head up, but another flash of lightning and immediate thunder and the poor woman covered her head with her arms again, and gave another small scream, 'aaaaaah!' The storm was overhead. I tried not to feel that I myself was being singled out for instant annihilation by a wrathful deity.

After a moment of silence, apart from the battering rain, the woman lowered her arms and raised her head cautiously. Seeing no more lightning for that instant she went on, her voice raised against the noise of the rain: "I think it is good to live that time because you do nothing except you ask first the gods if it is good. You ask the oak tree, you watch the birds how they fly. I like very much to live that time because the gods they are everywhere, and you do the right thing and they too, they help you, no?"

Her husband asked: "And you? You are staying in Ioannina?" Again there was a flash of lightning and cracking thunder, and his wife dived for cover under her arms, letting out another piteous scream: 'aaaaaah!'

I pretended not to care. "Only for tonight. Tomorrow we're going on to Meteora, then Litochoro and we end up in Salonika," I shouted.

"Ah, then at Salonika you will visit the museum and see the treasures from Philip II's tomb," the husband shouted back.

"I hope so."

Flash of lightning, but now there was a short pause before the thunder. The storm was moving on. The wife kept her head lowered and, after a while, peered up fearfully. "It is going?" she asked.

"The worst is over," I assured her.

"Ah, how I hate the thunder! How I hate the lightning!" she said. She raised her head higher to survey the scene. The ominous darkness was rolling on over the mountains, and it was getting lighter.

"And you?" I asked. "Are you staying in Ioannina?"

"Yes, we stay there." She sat upright once again with confidence. "We like very much to walk in the mountains," she said. "The Zagorohória villages, they are very nice."

As an enthusiast on old legends the Dutch woman told me how it was claimed that the ship, the Argo, in which Jason had set out to find the golden fleece, had had in its keel a plank of wood from the sacred oak at Dodona. "This wood, it is put in the boat by the goddess Athena to keep safe from danger the ship and the men in her," she said. "As the wood it is from the sacred oak of Zeus, the boat it speaks to tell Jason what he must next to do. They say also there is in the Argo a man who comes from Dodona, who looks to see how the birds they fly, and this also tells to him if it is good for Jason to do this, or to do that."

Harry and the Dutchman were now into a discussion about thunderstorms. "You'd never think that clouds colliding could cause electrical discharges producing lightning and thunder," Harry remarked. "After all, clouds are only vapour." He had no sense of divine vengeance.

"It is interesting how the vapour which becomes rain-drops contains electricity," said the Dutchman.

"But if you were up there in the cloud it would swirl around you and you'd feel nothing," went on Harry. The discussion continued in a scientifically factual manner, soundly knocking on the head all wild imaginings.

The rain stopped as suddenly as it had started, and the sun shone causing steam to rise from the bonnet of the car. My fears that this thunderstorm had been expressly sent to destroy me waned now the threat of being struck by lightning had gone. My master plan for this journey could continue.

METEORA - MT. OLYMPUS - SALONIKA

CHAPTER 5

SALONIKA

The bus station was a seething mass of people travelling for their various reasons across the northern mountainous landmass. I watched old men with gnarled sticks, and aged women with black scarves over their heads. What a bustle as buses arrived and departed. Many people carried heavy packages or suit-cases. All were enquiring, all were in transit. I could see a heavily pregnant woman seated nearby; she had on a red, black and yellow chequered woollen skirt, with a black apron edged with embroidery, and wore a Paisley-patterned head scarf in red, yellow and blue-grey.

I consulted a young Greek woman beside me who said she was making the same journey and, yes, we were waiting for the right bus. When we got on board the woman checked our ticket numbers and showed us where to sit.

We were confident we were seated correctly, which was just as well because a small rumpus was brewing. It appeared that two tickets had been issued for seat number four. The row crescendoed suddenly - the Greeks are vociferous when they believe they have a right to something. In an instant the shouting had gone from loud to double fortissimo.

Harry's ticket was examined by the conductor because some man was accusing him of sitting in his seat. Harry stayed immobile, and put on an expression of I-am-a-British-citizen-and-do-not-speak-to-angry-foreigners. I suspected that the would-be usurper of Harry's seat was picking on him because he was obviously not Greek.

As swiftly as he'd accosted Harry, he switched his attention to a mild and meek fellow across the aisle, and demanded his seat. Several men on board joined in this cacophony of male outrage. In contrast, a beautiful young girl sat beyond, outwardly quite calm, but comforting herself by twisting a strand of her long, dark hair round and round her index finger.

The would-be usurper of a seat suddenly, and without warning, marched towards the front of the bus and placed himself firmly beside the driver in the conductor's seat. There he sat immovably, arms crossed. The conductor poured out abuse, but the usurper of his seat was more abusive and remained in situ. It was clear that if the journey was to take place it would be best to leave the usurper where he was, and this the conductor sensibly decided to do.

But still we were not off. As the beautiful girl continued to twist her hair soothingly around her finger, an unshaven, plump young fellow came forward from the rear, and stood facing us would-be travellers. Under his left arm he clutched a black zipped brief-case, in his right he held up a large box of matches with a picture of the Virgin Mary on it, and made a holy proclamation. As we were hoping to travel to Kalambaka, to the Meteora monasteries, this was

I supposed appropriate to the holiness of this trip.

It was too much for the conductor, however, who told him sharply to shut-up and go back to his seat. At the same moment an Orthodox priest, who had been standing at the entrance to the bus watching gravely, showed extreme anxiety. But the bus door was slammed shut in his face and the poor priest moved away looking sorrowful.

Rather surprisingly, throughout the whole journey to Kalambaka, during which the conductor stood and the usurper of his seat sat comfortably, the two of them, together with the driver, appeared to be the best of friends, all grievances forgotten. In fact, the usurper of the conductor's seat became the life and soul of the journey and seemed never to be without some new thought springing to his mind. The driver was the most cautious one we had ever had the good fortune to be driven by. So slow and so careful was he that we wished he would go faster. But we were exceedingly glad to be in his care because the road was treacherous with yawning chasms and sheer precipices; mountain after mountain had to be negotiated. When he spotted a lorry coming from the opposite direction, he would wait in a lay-by until it appeared around the hairpin bend and had passed us. He himself never took such corners except in the lowest of low gears. It took a little getting used to seeing the front of the bus over the side of the precipice, its wheels being well back from the front. Yet, even on a straight road with solid ground on either side, he still crawled; and all the while the usurper quipped and continued a lively commentary for the four hour journey to Kalambaka (a journey which should take far less time).

As we approached the town we came down into a wide plain containing strange dollops of dark volcanic rock. The first rocks seemed to greet us like a welcoming party; they had rock heads perched on rock bodies with cavities in them like smiling mouths. It was strange driving down into this landscape. It was almost as though we were fish swimming in a marine world, in and out amongst gigantic rocks weathered by the tides, except that the waters had receded, leaving these smiling figures stranded on dry land. Soon we saw the first pinnacle with a monastery perched on top. These famous Meteora monasteries were built, not on ancient pagan sites, but on hundred-feet-high, sheer precipitous rock formations. To be nearer to God had been the ambition of the first ascetics who'd taken up their abode on them.

I had read that it was possible to stay as a guest at one of the monasteries but hadn't known that, in fact, an introductory letter was required. The result was that when I asked about it (Harry was happily unaware of my enquiry in Greek), and was politely refused, the rejection became a whetter of my appetite. There was a seductive charm and attraction about the place and, the more I saw, the more determined I became to return, not as a tourist but as a guest one day.

"Would you like to stay with the nuns at the Agios Stephanos?" I asked Harry. We were watching a large container being winched across a chasm along a steel cable, slowly making its way from the road to the Monastery of Agia Triada (Holy Trinity) perched on its rock.

"Why on earth would I want to do that?" came the positive response.

"To wake up on a pinnacle of rock would be, well, different - an adventure."

"I can think of better adventures, thank you," was the predictable reply.

In other words, it was up to me to do it alone or with a friend if I really wanted to. We ourselves were heading on to Mt. Olympus where, on this our second visit, I secretly hoped to climb up to the Mytikas Peak.

My spirits rose as the bus approached Litochoro, the small garrison town at the foot of Mt. Olympus. We were going back to the same family-run hotel in which we'd stayed before, and I was looking forward to meeting the hotel manager and his wife again. But it turned out to be a sad occasion. Instead of cheerful greetings, we found the family plunged in misery. The manager's wife had died the previous year, leaving the poor man desolate and speechless with grief. His daughter was now running the place. Her father had become incapable of doing anything but the lightest of tasks; he pulled the curtains at night and drew them back in the morning, and ran small errands; he was otherwise quite at a loss in his bereavement.

We walked out and up the steep and narrow road to the top of Litochoro to try to shake off this shroud of unexpected gloom.

"Will you go to pieces when I'm gone?" I asked Harry.

"Life goes on," he remarked in one of his evasive won't-think-about-it tones, which could either imply that he would struggle on in misery, or life could begin again to his advantage. Fortunately, before I could quizz him on the matter, this talk of death was interrupted by a cheerful procession of bride and groom, together with their guests, streaming down the hill from around a corner. Our shroud of mourning was immediately tossed aside as these revellers came joyfully down the narrow road.

Yes, life went on.

Early next morning found us sitting on our hotel balcony peacefully contemplating the mountain. The early morning light was astonishingly bright, and every crag and cranny on the mountain appeared sharply delineated. There wasn't a cloud in the sky. Near the summit, and clearly visible, I saw a broad scallop-shaped rock against the skyline. I recognized it from pictures as the Throne of Zeus. Harry was scathingly dismissive: there must be hundreds of possible 'thrones' up there, he said. Every large rock could be a 'throne'. I wasn't discouraged. That huge, scallop-shaped rock, pinkly suffused in the dawn light was, undoubtedly, the Throne of Zeus. I felt I was being favoured with a sighting and it was a good omen.

I'd delayed saying anything to Harry about climbing to the Mytikas Peak and the Throne of Zeus as I'd been waiting for the right moment. So far no 'right moment' had presented itself. Clearly I had to grasp the nettle now as we had to climb that day or not at all.

"It would be nice to get up to the top this time," I said nonchalantly.

"Top of what?" Harry was suspicious.

"The mountain," I replied.

"You mean Olympus?"

"Yes."

"You mean climb it again?"

"Well, we can't fly it," I murmured.

"Absolutely not!" came the decisive response. "We tried it once and failed. No fear!"

I knew from his tone I had no hope of changing his mind, and was ashamed at how pleased I was to hear this response. In my mind I was courageous, but in reality I hated heights and chasms. I said meekly: "Well, I take it you don't mind walking on the lower slopes?" A grunt was the best I could expect under the circumstances, and I took it to mean yes.

It was a good day for walking. My plan was to hike from the Monastery of Dionysios back to Litochoro. We took a taxi to the monastery amidst a certain amount of grumbling about expense; but I pointed out that it would be better to start there and walk back, than to start here and pick up on the wrong track, get lost, and have to spend the night out on the mountain sleeping rough.

The monastery stood in a forest clearing with the mountain peaks behind it rising steeply to the deep blue sky. This year we found its church being rebuilt, the original having been destroyed by the Germans during World War II. We entered the bare-walled building, and I lit a candle before a solitary icon of Agios Dionysios. His elderly, watchful eyes, above his long grey beard, stared back - rather accusingly, I thought. I had a theory that the saint's presence on the mountain was due to the old pagan god Dionysos who'd been worshipped on these lower slopes. To establish a monastery dedicated to St. Dionysios seemed to me a clear attempt to ease any latent pagan worship into the new Christian mould.

A forest worker pointed out the track which would take us back to Litochoro. He looked dubious when I told him we intended to walk the whole way but, being keen to do it, I dimissed the thought there might be problems.

After less than a hundred yards or so we came to a grassy glade where several Greek families sat picnicking beside the shallow river Epineas. Here it flowed and rippled over small boulders which were used as stepping stones to reach the other side. We crossed the river and followed a narrow foot-path which very occasionally was marked by a red splodge painted on a tree or, more rarely, a yellow metal square pinned to it with E4 stamped on it. This E4 route, we learned later, began in the Pyrenees and ended in the Peloponnese near to Sparta.

About fifteen minutes on we came across a tiny chapel within an overhang of rock. There were many newly lighted candles outside its low entrance. We supposed that it was from this shrine that the families we'd seen seated by the river had come. There were signs of habitation but we saw no one.

The rock-floor of this little chapel had a wide crevice through which we could see the mountain stream tumbling away to the river below. We wondered whether these waters were known to have healing qualities, and whether people came and lit candles there for the cure of ailments.

We continued on our way, passing through a forest of conifers and following a track carpeted by pine-needles. Occasionally, we glimsed beech trees in their glorious autumn colours on the lower slopes. Here and there were clumps of cyclamen and the occasional yellow autumn crocus.

At times we were high above the gorge with the river way below tumbling over boulders and precipices. I avoided looking down because it made me dizzy to see this thin strip of tumultuous flowing water so far below. At other times we had to descend steeply, going backwards and hanging on to exposed roots and branches. Such places were sometimes made more passable by pine logs pinned into position by metal pegs, thus making steps here and there. Occasionally, we had to haul ourselves up a steep incline by catching hold of whatever we could grab at. There was the occasional fallen tree across our path which we either had to climb over or pass under. At one point the mountain side was rough scree whose volcanic grey made a perfect background to the brilliant autumn colours of many smoke bushes growing there.

As the hours passed, I became fearful that the next crest would find us faced with a yawning chasm, and we would have to retrace our steps; or that the landslip of shale and scree under which the track became hidden, and across which we had to pass, would begin to slip away under our weight, taking us with it.

We did a steep down-on-our-behinds stretch until, quite unexpectedly, we found ourselves beside the river looking at a natural grotto. The water here was pale green, clear as glass, still and silent and overhung by ferns and wild grasses. The mountainous back-drop of pine trees soared upwards to the blue sky. There was no sound except for a bird whistling from a nearby bush, and the gentle rippling of water around the boulder on which we sat mid-stream.

"Throne of Zoos!" Harry remarked, pointing to a gigantic rock with perpendicular fluting. This was the third time he'd pointed to a so-called 'throne'. I said that from the size of it it was more likely to be a throne of Hera; and anyway the thrones of the gods had been made of gold, not rock. This, of course, brought Harry's immediate retort that in that case my so called 'throne' that morning was nothing but a sham.

Because Harry was taunting me with 'thrones', I took up the 'throne' cudgels and told him a 'throne' story. It was about Hephaestus, the lame son of Hera, who had once been so furious with his mother on Mt. Olympus, that he'd constructed a gold throne for her - yes, gold, not rock - which had had a secret device hidden in it. This, when she'd sat down, had pinioned her to her seat, and none of the immortals had been able to release her. It had eventually been Dionysos who'd obtained Hera's release. By entertaining Hephaestus, paying him compliments, getting him drunk on wine, and promising him Aphrodite for his wife, Dionysos had cunningly persuaded him of his great standing in the immortal world. He had then led him back to Mt. Olympus on a mule, with all the Olympians lining the route and cheering him. This had so flattered and pleased Hephaestus, that he'd immediately released his mother and then, as promised, had been married to Aphrodite.

Mt. Olympus abounded with such stories. The presence of the gods was almost tangible. There was the one about Tiresias who had surprised Athena bathing naked in just such a pool as the one we were now looking at. Athena's reaction had been to raise her hands to cover, not her nakedness, but Tiresias' eyes which had immediately blinded him. To make up for this misfortune, Athena granted the poor man the gift of prophecy, and the ability to understand the speech of birds. She also gave him a miraculous staff which guided him as though he still had his sight. It was Tiresias who'd warned the young and arrogant Pentheus, king of Thebes, not to scoff at Dionysos who'd arrived at his court, but to honour him as an immortal god. But Pentheus had paid no attention, and had consequently been torn to pieces for his disbelief.

I remembered another story which seemed appropriate to sitting there mid-river. It was about Orpheus, the legendary pre-Homeric mystic, musician and poet. Orpheus had been famed for his singing and his ability to tame wild animals. For some reason, however, he had also refused to honour Dionysos here on Mt. Olympus, and the women devotees of the god had been so irate they'd torn Orpheus limb from limb, buried him at the base of the mountain, and had finally thrown his head into some river (not the Epineas) where it had floated, still singing, to the sea.

"Singing?" queried Harry. "Not screaming?" He tossed a dry twig into the eddying waters and watched it sail away, its dark shadow moving swiftly over the pebbles of the river-bed.

I ignored the question. "Orpheus was another one who sailed with the Argonauts to help Jason retrieve the golden fleece," I said.

"Everyone seems to have sailed with Jason," Harry remarked.

"It was Orpheus who saved the Argonauts from the Siren voices," I went on. "The Sirens were weird women who lured sailors to their certain deaths by their magical singing. But, because Orpheus sang more magically, and especially at that particular moment when passing them, his fellow Argonauts kept on course whilst the Siren voices desperately tried but failed to get them to change direction."

"Well, his magical voice didn't charm the women who murdered him," Harry said, and he threw another dry twig into the river, and watched it race and swirl away chased by its shadow on the river-bed.

I wished we could stay for ever idling by this sacred grotto but, before rigor mortis set in irredeemably (I could already feel my legs stiffening up) it was imperative to move on - to leave this whatever-one-could-call-it and words would still be inadequate.

We searched for the trail onwards but every possible track led into a thicket, and we had to retrace our steps. At last Harry caught sight of a splodge of red paint on the trunk of a tree the other side of the river, and we crossed over, using boulders as stepping-stones. Not long afterwards we met up with four young people who had come up from the youth hostel some hours away. It was extraordinarily reassuring to know there were other human beings on this mountain. Although solitude is something to be enjoyed, human contact is also necessary after having been deprived of it for a while. These young students warned us that the river had to be crossed another three times, twice where it was shallow and once where it was - well, tricky. They also looked dubious as to our capacity to do it.

We got over the two shallow crossings easily, then came to the deep one. Here the river was fast flowing, and the large boulders were inconveniently apart. The first two were relatively easy to jump to, and we sat on the second and watched the river swirl and flow swiftly on before cascading away to somewhere which, from the sound of it, was a precipitous drop not many yards away.

Harry decided he had to take command which meant standing up and considering his options. Either we could jump to the next boulder, and possibly land in the rapids and have to swim for it - well, Harry would, I'd just drown; or we could turn and walk the four hours back again; or we could stay put. He wasn't turning back or staying put so, donning an ill-fitting Tarzan hat, he took a flying leap to the next boulder where he landed on one leg with both arms flailing before he regained his balance. He then turned and stretched out an arm towards me.

"Get a grip!" he commanded. His hand was about six inches short of mine, and I wasn't going to jump and hope he'd grab me in mid air.

No way! Far from getting me across I knew I would quite certainly unbalance him, and we would both be swept away to oblivion. I wasn't going to risk being shot over that waterfall.

We stood helplessly on our two boulders wondering how to get out of our predicament when, quite unexpectedly, a young man appeared on the other bank and began springing from boulder to boulder towards us. The young stalwart first helped Harry across, then nimbly leaped back to get me. He held out a strong arm which appeared twice the length of Harry's, and grasped my hand; he stood solid as a young tree rooted to his boulder as I sprang through the air. I landed with one leg in the water anyway, but was hauled out with effuse apologies.

"He had to be a god!" I told Harry when we'd parted from him. "He had to be Dionysos, god, or Dionysios, saint."

Harry merely commented that, as he hadn't got a long grey beard, he was clearly not the saint. "He was there because he was walking the same route in the opposite direction, that's all!" he declared.

"God, you're so unimaginative!"

"It's just as well one of us has his head screwed on," came the reply.

As we got lower and lower down the mountain, the gorge widened. Another hour passed and we heard a human voice, only faintly as yet, but a surprisingly welcome sound. Then, in the distance we saw a figure sitting on a rock.

"Zoos sitting on his throne!" Harry proclaimed.

I ignored the jibe. When we at last reached the spot we found three youths who told us that we could expect to get to Litochoro in about an hour. Another hour?

It was nice to know that there were more people behind as well as ahead of us. If one of us slipped and broke a leg, help was not too far away.

Not long after parting from the group, we heard one of the young men shouting up at the mountain. His voice reverberated and echoed repeatedly around the caves, gorges and mountain peaks. Then we crested a ridge, and there at last we looked down over Litochoro and saw the wide sweep of estuary beyond stretching away down to the sea. We were elated. Our trek through god territory had lasted six hours.

We tramped back to our hotel like automatons, and lay flat on our backs for the rest of the day. Even with my eyes closed I kept seeing footpaths and boulders and precipices and waterfalls, and it was a long while before my legs had stopped walking.

Travelling by night is a marvellously unstressful way of making the long journey through the hazardous mountain passes. As I could see nothing I abandoned myself to my Fate, to those Moirai of old who spun the threads of life – and death. We were on our way back to Corfu having spent several days in Salonika.

"Have a boiled sweet?" Harry offered. It was his way of preventing travel sickness. Any such symptoms suggested to me a terminal collapse of good health. I tossed about on my seat, trying to settle myself into a comfortable position, and finished curled up like a dog too large for its basket. I couldn't sleep as the activities of the last few days filled my mind; I'd found the hubbub of Salonika stimulating.

Salonika, city of St. Paul! St. Paul, who wrote his two short Epistles to the Thessalonians, and warned them to 'abstain from immorality'. Whilst there, we'd visited the early churches, starting with the beautiful fifth century basilica church dedicated to the patron saint of the city, Agios Demetrios.

The intention of those who'd built the early churches had been to give the worshippers a vision of heaven on earth; to enrich the human senses - sight, hearing, smell, taste and touch. They used marble columns, as in the pagan temples, to draw the eye up to the great dome above richly decorated with mosaics.

When in 324 A.D. the Emperor Constantine acknowledged Christianity as a true religion, the Christians of Salonika had hastened to honour the martyr Demetrios, by building a small church on the site where it was believed his martyrdom had taken place. This became the focal point for pilgrims seeking cures.

My real interest was in the name Demetrios which was the male version of Demeter. St. Demetrios was regarded as a warrior saint but, as patron saint of the city, the people would have looked to him for protection as much against famine and bad harvests as against invaders. How much of a coincidence was it that the saint's feast-day is in the autumn, the time that the Greater Mysteries of the old goddess had been? In truth little, if anything, is known of the saint and his legend grew as though by magic.

We had also visited the early church of Agia Sophia (Holy Wisdom). In the apse above the sanctuary was a wonderful mosaic of the Virgin and Child. I had read that originally it had been the Virgin alone holding a cross. To a pagan teetering on the edge of Christianity such a figure might have been thought of as Athena, the old goddess of wisdom, with a cross held for all to see. Later the figure of the child replaced the cross which equally could have been the goddess Demeter with the baby Persephone on her lap.

In the central dome of Agia Sophia was a mosaic representation of Christ's Ascension, made visible by the light slanting in from the twelve arched windows in the square base on which the dome rested. It portrayed Christ being lifted up by two angels. The angels were interesting because the day before we had visited the wonderful Archaeological Museum of Salonika. There I had paused before a statue thought to be of the second century Emperor Hadrian. On his armour had been figures with huge deep wings which I had at first taken to be angels crowning him emperor. I'd retrieved myself from being quite witless when I realized that a pagan emperor would never have had angels crowning him and that these were, in fact, pagan representations of Nike (Victory). I have since learned that the Greek winged figure of Victory came long before early representations of angels. The word 'angelos' is Greek for messenger, and these first messengers of God in the Old Testament had been without wings. So here, in the dome of Agia Sophia were angels raising Christ to heaven which, to lingering pagan eyes, would have represented Nikes, or the visual triumph of Christ's 'victory' over death.

We'd spent time at the Byzantine and early Christian Museum in the White Tower in Salonika, a sixteenth century construction. There we'd seen early Christian artefacts such as seals, coins, icons and suchlike. Each floor was reached by climbing the shallow steps spiralling around the tower.

The floor which exhibited burial customs portraying

the overlap from pagan to Christian belief had been startling. In the early years, when Christianity was being established in Greece, it had been impossible to abolish ancient customs overnight, especially those regarding death and burial. Considering the emotional upset caused by death, it is easy to understand how the bereaved in a family would have held on stubbornly to the customs of their forebears. To those still faithful to the pagan gods under the new Christian empire, it had remained obligatory to send the body on its way with the same care and attention as before. It had always been the custom to place a coin on the tongue of the deceased as payment to Charon, the ferryman who, it was believed, ferried the dead across the River Styx to the shadowy world of Hades. The idea of Charon did not die out with the end of paganism; instead, Charon became the symbol of Death personified.

In the museum there had been a tomb painting of Charon ferrying his latest victim across the Styx - dated between the third and fifth century A.D. The fish on the tomb painting could have been regarded either as natural to the river scene, or recognisable as the secret symbol of a Christian in times of persecution. The fish had become the symbol because the Greek for fish was 'Ixthus', and these letters composed the initials of the words 'Jesus Christ, Son of God, Saviour' (Iesous Xristos Theou Uios Soteir).

There were many coins on display taken from these early Christian graves, together with bowls and cups and such things from which the deceased was believed to feed and drink to sustain him through his after life.

There was no change either in the tradition of providing the dead with food both at the time of the funeral and afterwards. It is still a tradition which goes back into antiquity long before Christ. Today in Greece there is the funeral feast for those assembled at the grave side. At fixed intervals subsequently the same thing is repeated; the food prepared is known as kollyva and consists of mixed grain, symbolic of the burial of seed and its resurrection.

Travelling by night was a pleasure, dozing on and off as I did, whilst the bus groped its way through the mountain passes, sometimes through dense cloud, sometimes with clear patches when I could see a spread of lights in a valley or a mushroom shape of lights up the side of the mountain. Way, way beyond I sometimes saw the headlights of a car or lorry, but how we passed it was something that failed to concern me as I could not see the hazards, or whether the driver was nodding off to sleep or not. I supposed the bus at some point would be passing Mt. Olympus, and Meteora.

I could see no moon that night. In Salonika, on our return from the Archaeological Museum where, as advised, we had seen the exquisite gold artefacts from the tomb of Philip II (father of Alexander the Great), we had stopped off at a taverna on the sea front. It had been growing dark, and all around the bay were the twinkling lights of the city, and in harbour the ships were lit up. Suddenly I had noticed low on the horizon where the sea was being whipped up by the wind into small choppy wavelets, the finest of crescent moons, as fine as any treasure of burnished gold from the Macedonian tomb.

It is interesting that, like Christ who died and rose again on the third day, the moon also seems to die and is not to be seen for two days before reappearing as though resurrected from the dead on the third.

It was dawn when the bus arrived at Igoumenitsa the small port on the north-west coast of Greece. Here, other overnight buses were converging from different parts of

Greece. I wished there was time to visit the Nekromanteion of Ephyra a few miles south along the coast, where the two women I met at Eleusis were going. There, legend had it that Orpheus went down to Hades to rescue his beloved young bride, Eurydice. At the site today are the ancient remains of the oracle of the dead and a sanctuary of Persephone and Hades. It is, apparently, a labyrinthian construction of corridors and windowless rooms. In Homer's Odyssey, Odysseus was said to have made contact with the dead by coming to this place. There he revived the 'strengthless presences of the dead' by pouring libations 'first with milk and honey, then with sweet wine, then with water', and finally by sprinkling 'white barley-meal'.

But there was no time to visit this mysterious site, this entry to the world of Hades. My mind had to return to things of the present, not things of the past. Harry had excelled himself in keeping up with me and now he was already sniffing the air, smelling freedom and the end of tramping around churches and ancient archaeological sites.

"I'll buy a bottle of whisky at the duty-free," he remarked. "I might get some cigars, they'll make good Christmas presents." And a moment later: "Don't let me forget that I've the vet coming on Monday to de-horn our animals." The streams of thought were already dragging at me; the pull of the tide of home-coming was drawing me back into the strong undertow of commitments at home.

It was dark when our flight was called and it was drizzling as we crossed the tarmac to our plane. Harry, with a happy smile at the thought of soon being home

6

METEORA

"What is your address here in Kalambaka?" asked the receptionist. I and a friend we called the Stoic had only just arrived off the bus, and we were changing travellers cheques at a hotel. A public holiday was coming up, the banks were already closed and I was running out of money. The Stoic, as her name implies, was stoical but better still she was always game for anything and never tired. She lived in Cyprus, and had driven with us around the Greek part of the island when we'd been there.

"The Agios Stephanos, Meteora," I replied.

The girl looked at me. "That is impossible," she said. "Nobody stays at those monasteries."

I had no intention of admitting defeat so early, and replied that certainly my friend and I hoped to stay there.

The taxi driver was as pessimistic as the hotel receptionist. There was no point in making the trip, he kept repeating, because the monasteries would be closing in twenty minutes. He had absolutely no faith whereas for once I had.

The grey-black rock formations behind Kalambaka were weird and challenging, rising as they did from the landscape. We saw our first monastery clinging like a barnacle to the top of its sheer faced rock. The first question most people asked was how did they build them there? My question was why did they build them there?

The taxi wound its way up a hill, then took a sharp left turn, and approached the Monastery of Agios Stephanos. A bridge spanned the chasm which separated the road from the monastery. An eagle, sacred to Zeus, circled high above the buildings, and I felt it to be a good omen. I asked the driver to wait whilst I went in to make enquiries.

The nun at the door smiled kindly when I told her I believed that I and a friend were expected, and we'd come to stay. No, she was sorry but they never took overnight visitors, she said. I told her that a letter of introduction had been sent on my behalf by a cousin of one of the nuns. I had, in fact, met the young woman at the Greek Tourist Office in London who'd arranged it for me. I said I was interested in Orthodoxy, and that I myself had written and had asked that they should let me know if they couldn't have me. Since I hadn't heard I'd supposed they were able to welcome me and my friend.

The nun picked up the phone and communed with a higher authority. She put the receiver back and, speaking kindly but firmly, told me again she was sorry but it was not permitted. I suppose I must have spoken as kindly and firmly back, although my Greek was rapidly forsaking me, because I stood my ground and repeated how I'd asked expressly for them to write if they couldn't have me and, as they'd failed to do so, naturally I'd supposed they were expecting us. Again the nun telephoned keeping one eye on me. I hoped I looked modest and suitably dressed, and a searcher after God. After several minutes of talk she put down the receiver and smiled sweetly. Permission had been granted and I and my friend could stay, she said.

I was elated. I had been on the point of accepting defeat but suddenly all opposition had been removed.

"We can stay? Hoorah!" said the Stoic. "You've been so long, dear, I thought you must be taking your vows. I was wondering how I could possibly tell Harry I'd lost you to the nuns."

The taxi driver's earlier pessimism quickly altered to one of respect and almost veneration for his two passengers who had this entrée to the monastery. He carried our luggage across the bridge, and shook hands on parting.

Any uncertainty as to what to do next, or how to behave, was quickly dispersed by two young nuns who were sent to make us welcome. We were greeted and kissed on both cheeks; they were so happy and pleased to have us, they said.

We were taken along a quadrangle to the guest wing where a door marked 'private' was opened for us. Were we hungry? What would we like to eat? I asked if we could have a cup of tea. A five hour journey, three changes of bus and my anxieties and efforts to come to them had left me drained. We were told that tea would be prepared, and someone would knock on our door when it was ready.

Beyond the net curtain to our window we could see the shadowy figures of the last of the tourists as they made their way out along the cloisters to the exit.

"Well!" said the Stoic, when we were left to ourselves. "This is a cut above the refuge-hut up Mt. Olympus!" Not having Harry with me had given me the opportunity I'd wanted to try a second attempt to scale the mountain of the gods. But my ambition to reach the Throne of Zeus had, as on the first occasion, been thwarted, as once again clouds had closed in and it had rained all night; by morning the refuge-hut had been shrouded in a dense white fog. The Stoic had said: "Well, I'm in your hands, dear. If you want to get higher in the fog, we'll do it. If you want to go on to Meteora then that's fine by me." As there were certain dead-lines to be met, I'd settled for the latter with some relief.

Our room was sparsely furnished with dormitory type beds, a table with a cloth embroidered with crosses, and a rush-seated chair and wardrobe. Above the beds were two icons, one of the Virgin and Child and one of Christ Pantokrator.

"Did you have great difficulty in persuading them to let us stay?" asked the Stoic, as she unpacked her things for the night.

"Yes, great difficulty," I replied.

"How come you won the day?"

"I don't know. I thought I'd failed and suddenly - " I shrugged. I felt peculiarly humble and holy.

"Don't go getting a conversion on me," warned the Stoic. "I really wouldn't know how to handle you if you got God in a big way."

"I wouldn't know how to handle myself. But we're very privileged," I replied. I had an odd feeling that there was something outside my control working for me.

We were about to revive ourselves with our own private supply of biscuits when there was a knock at the door. The face of the Sister in charge of our welfare beamed at us from the doorway. Tea was ready, she said. We followed the small, sturdy figure as she led the way to her kitchen and the dining-room beyond. The table was laid with a plate of French toast, butter, a large bowl of honey, mountain tea

(tea made from herbs gathered from the mountain) and a segment of crystallized orange each.

"My goodness, they do us proud," commented the Stoic. "I can't believe we're here!" she said. "What on earth gave you the idea?"

"I don't know. What gives anyone an idea?" I asked.

While we ate we were visited by the Abbess. She was a tiny figure in black with a gentle, serene face. She gave me a long searching look, and I feared she sensed the pagan in me. A young novice helped to interpret. I told her I was interested in Orthodoxy and we hoped to join in their services. Certainly we could do that, she said. Could we also, I asked, see the studio where they painted icons, something for which I'd heard they were famous?

The Abbess replied quietly that first she must bless the room. This meant, said the novice, that she would see if it was the will of God.

We were told we could wander wherever we liked, and that Vespers would be held at six-thirty. The Sister would provide us with supper after that.

We had time to spare before Vespers and wandered out along the cloisters to a terrace where a nun was busy watering terracotta pots of plants. From there we were able to look down over the sheer-faced rock to the wide plain far below. There we could see the river Pineus winding its way like a thin lead ribbon; the main road stretched straight as a ruler far into the distance with toy-like cars and lorries speeding in both directions. The town of Kalambaka fanned itself beyond like a scattering of children's building blocks. Life with all its modern pressures and anxieties erupted down there, whilst up in our rock monastery we were ringed around by an aura of peace.

I told the Stoic how ancient legend claimed that this

area had once been an inland sea, and that Poseidon, god of earthquakes as well as the sea, had caused a great upheaval so that the waters had drained into the Aegean, exposing these strange rock formations.

"Well, it makes a convincing story," agreed the Stoic.

"But the monks think that they are the result of the great flood of Noah's time," I went on. "They believe the rocks were deposited here by the Almighty for the express purpose for monks to build monasteries on them."

"Well, people think whatever fits the bill, I suppose," mused the Stoic.

The ancient Greeks had, apparently, shown no interest in this inland terrain with its inhospitable pinnacles of rock. But to dedicated Christians, when they became troubled by Turkish occupation in the fifteenth century, these rocks were a means of isolating themselves; somewhere they could live in perpetual prayer high above humanity, mediating between the sins of the world and God.

As we peered down from our rock the Stoic said: "Enlighten me, do! How in heaven's name did the first monks get themselves up? Were they athletes? Olympic gymnasts?"

"Well, one theory is that the monk Athanasius - the first ascetic to live on one of them - was brought up on the back of an eagle," I said.

"Well, having got here on his eagle, how about food? How about drink?" Her questions flowed thick and fast. "Did anybody know he'd been deposited up a rock by an eagle? Did anybody miss him?"

"Well, another theory suggested by some Patriarch in the sixteenth century was that he was borne up by the wings of the Holy Spirit," I said.

"Does the Holy Spirit have wings?" the Stoic asked.

"The Holy Spirit is uplifting and, therefore, can help you to fly," I said vaguely.

I had, in fact, timed this Meteora trip to coincide with the Orthodox Pentecost (the coming of the Holy Spirit), an important celebration in the Orthodox Church. A holy spirit - maybe THE Holy Spirit was something about which I felt fairly positive. The following day would be the eve of Pentecost.

"It's as well to feel positive about something," said the Stoic when I told her this. "I only feel positive about myself. 'I think, therefore I am', a sort of Descartian philosophy."

"Don't you have a sense of the holy up here?"

"You mean a nearer to God feel? As an atheist, dear, I can't say that I do. But don't let me stop you on your search for your great God," she said.

"The Abbess asks if you would like to walk with us outside and we will tell you about the Orthodox Church," a young novice said after Vespers. "There are two of us who speak English and will accompany you."

We crossed the bridge to the hill of Koukoulas. It was a fine, still evening with a large full moon rising above a volcanic looking sugar-loaf pinnacle to the east. To the west the sun was setting behind the rocks; the lights of Kalambaka twinkled far below. There was no traffic on our road, and nobody about except for a solitary silhouetted figure against the skyline. It was a young man on a dollop of rock performing Tai Chi to the setting sun. In slow motion this small ant-like figure raised one arm, then a leg and elongated or contracted his whole body as he made his devotions to the powers that be. Our two nuns cheerfully told us that such a thing was frowned upon as it was considered egotistical; the man was seeking peace for himself rather than finding it through God and radiating it out to others.

We walked along the deserted road. I was surprised at how cheerful and uncomplicated our young novices were. Their body language and enthusiasm didn't fit with my idea of nuns who, I supposed, would walk demurely with their hands clasped. Our two seemed to dance along in their flat sandals beside us, bubbling with information and answering any question without hesitation. One of them was Australian and in her late twenties.

I asked them what had brought them to convent life. They had been unable to ignore the call of God, they said. "How do you know when God calls you?" I asked.

"You have this overflowing love in your heart," came the instant reply from the Australian. She told us how she had formerly been teaching English in Athens; there she'd been drawn to the Orthodox Church, and had eventually been baptized into it. She described the overwhelming experience after her total immersion (required at baptism in the Orthodox Church) when she had felt possessed by the Holy Spirit. She had subsequently come every weekend to Meteora, and it had been a natural progression for her to enter convent life. As yet still a novice, she was certain she would stay the course, and was supremely happy at the thought of being accepted fully as a nun and remaining there for life.

The other told us how she had nearly completed her three years as a novice and hoped in a month's time to become a Sister. All depended on the Abbess who had to approve her advancement.

Every two months she confessed to her Spiritual

Father who guided her. Confessed? What sort of things did she confess, I asked? I was thinking of the shame or embarrassment of admitting sexual sins. It was surprisingly difficult to practise humility, she answered. For instance, she sang in the choir but must never think she sang better than the others. Or when she was asked to do more tasks than she thought fair, she must do them willingly. The devil was always entering their thoughts and trying to tempt them to stray from the true path. Humility and total obedience were hard to achieve, she said.

Was I thinking of being baptized into Orthodoxy, I was asked? (What me, an agnostic?) And yet I had wondered about it. I could take the plunge - that leap of faith. But was it a good enough reason that I would only be baptized into Orthodoxy because I heartily disliked listening to words in the Church of England which I could understand, but whose message I couldn't comprehend, and so preferred the incomprehensible in a foreign language? Or that I liked the way the Orthodox Church worked on the five senses, and preferred it to the Church of England which knocked most of my senses stone dead?

I told them what I knew to be true, that if I was ever baptized into the Orthodox Church Harry would feel I was going somewhat over the top in this spiritual search; he'd say that for a sceptic the Church of England was perfectly good enough. The young novices smiled tolerantly. Obviously if I felt really strongly, if it was the will of God, Harry would have to accept it. As it was, I clearly wasn't sufficiently sucked in. My very limited belief in a holy something - and also in the power of the mind - were things I could believe in any Church, or in no Church at all for that matter.

Inevitably I asked them about death and what they

thought happened. They were very positive. When you died your soul remained for three days with those you loved, after which it was taken by your guardian angel to a higher place where he pleaded for you. At the same time the devils tried to get hold of your soul. It was a frightening experience because you were in limbo whilst your guardian angel struggled to keep your soul from the devils. After that you either went higher towards God, or down to hell where all those who were similarly unfortunate were compressed together. Only by intercession from the Orthodox Church and the mention of your name, could your soul obtain fractional relief from this claustrophobic condition.

After what they said I had to admit that my own previously held belief, that death would be a good long sleep without any nightmarish devils tussling with my soul, was a far more attractive prospect. Or was it? Surely there'd be a reawakening in due course?

We began to wander back. The lights of Kalambaka were more brilliant now that the sun had set. The moon was higher, and the darkening sky and strange landscape of rock monasteries were taking on a glazed aura in the moonlight.

Our companions said that when they prayed they did so to the Virgin Mary because she seemed to them more accessible than Christ, a closer and more sympathetic figure. That didn't mean their love for Christ was any less, but that they found the Virgin Mary more approachable.

As we crossed the bridge to Agios Stephanos the young novices told us that nobody stayed in the monastery as a rule. In fact, it was so unusual they could only put it down to it being the will of God. We were, indeed, blessed, they told us. Only members of their families were encouraged to come once in a while, in order to see that they themselves were not being kept there against their wishes. One reason why strangers were refused admittance was that once a woman had walked out in the night and had thrown herself off the rock. After that they were not prepared to accept the responsibility of having strangers.

They told us also of a distressed young German who had once threatened to throw himself off the bridge. He had, however, been persuaded against it by a priest who had remonstrated with him. The young German had then gone to America where he had made good, and had written to the nuns asking them to convey his thanks to the priest. They had asked him to describe the priest and his description had fitted no one known to them, only the great saint, Charalambos, to whom the Katholikon was dedicated. Such are the stuff of miracles.

We said goodnight and made our way to our room.

"Well," said the Stoic, "we are blessed! That gives us food for thought! But before I allow myself to turn religious, I must sleep on it. I've lived aloof from any belief for so long I'm wary of becoming dependent on the Almighty. Self is the only thing I can feel sure about!"

After all I'd been told that day, my mind was in turmoil. I feared I might see a ghost; might walk off the rock in the night; might be sent a sudden 'On the road to Damascus' blinding vision. In order to avoid any such complications in my life I took a strong sleeping pill and slid gently down the slope into a deep sleep, beyond the pull of any spirit, good or evil.

I awoke only briefly in response to the sound of a wooden semantron; it was being beaten with a hammer outside our window to summon the nuns to prayer at five a.m. This beating of the semantron (either wooden or metal) was, I'd been told, symbolic of Noah calling the animals into the ark to save them from the flood, and consequently from the sins of the world.

In the morning we were free to visit other monasteries. We went first to the most famous of them, the Great Meteoron, built on twelve acres known as the Broad Rock, two hundred and fifty metres high. This was the one founded by the monk Athanasius ('athanasia' means 'immortality'). He was the same Athanasius who had first lived as an ascetic in a cave on Mt. Athos (the Holy Mountain of Halkidhiki where no women are allowed) until he was driven from the peninsular by pirates.*

As we climbed the steep steps to the Great Meteoron, our way was blocked by a woman in need of a hip replacement who was struggling up in front of us, using somebody's arm and a walking-stick. Her efforts to make it to the top was a shining example of human determination against all the odds.

It gave me time to read the various homilies placed at strategic places up the many steps. That day I was feeling more receptive to the 'Lord Jesus have mercy on me' and suchlike notices. When I'd come with Harry I'd taken a strong aversion to the warnings threatening us with eternal damnation, and the emphasis on sin. By the time Harry and I had reached the entrance to the monastery, and had seen the frescoed warnings of the Day of Judgement, I had felt thoroughly mutinous.

I couldn't understand why God had put it into the minds of those early Christians to scale rocks and live in caves. And, if it had been his will, then why had it been?

* See Chapter 4 in Ye Gods! for an account of Mt. Athos

In the days of paganism men had appeased the gods with sacrifice according to their means and capacity, but had never tried anything so excessive as to eke out the rest of their days on the top of pillars or in other inaccessible places. Either it revealed that men had turned mad with zeal, or else the Almighty had. When I'd mentioned these dark thoughts to Harry, he'd said that my trouble was I saw things only from my own perspective. Why, if somebody thought it God's will, shouldn't the poor fellow live his life on top of a pillar?

"But why would it be God's will?" I'd argued. "Don't ask me," had been the immediate reply. "The main thing is that the poor chap thought it was and did it. It shows courage - perhaps I mean spirit - and that's why people came from miles to admire him." "I would have thought it showed a certain wonkiness in the head," I'd said. Harry had dismissed the subject saying that, as I obviously didn't understand, he didn't intend discussing it further.

I still didn't understand, and I asked the Stoic what she thought.

"I think it amazing," she said at once. "Amazing that people can be so possessed by whatever possesses them, that they can scale rocks and live like mice, scavenging for food. However possessed I was, dear, I could in no way scale one of these rocks," she said positively.

"So what about the back of an eagle story?"

"I wouldn't have thought an eagle capable of carrying a man, dear."

"Well then, the power of the Holy Spirit?"

"I believe more in a long rope with grappling-hooks. That would demand faith, if ever faith was demanded - I mean, of course, in the rope and the hooks."

I might be a hopeless sceptic but another's atheism

always drove me in the direction of belief. In my present more harmonious mood, having spent the night in the heart of the Orthodox fraternity, I had no rebellious thoughts such as I'd had on the previous visit with Harry, but instead took on board 'Most Holy Mother of God save us' and 'The Lord Jesus Christ Save us from our sins'. The Stoic's atheism jarred slightly on my poetic mood.

When we eventually entered the Katholikon (the main church of a monastery), the woman with the hip problem had made it and was seated in the church with a smile on her face. She stared happily at the beauty of the frescoes, icons, carved and gilded sanctuary screen and bishop's throne which was intricately inlaid with ivory and mother of pearl. Her serenity washed off on me; as someone once said, it wasn't Christian doctrine that converted people so much as the example of those who practised it.

We walked out to the monastery terrace where we could look over this landscape of molar teeth and ravines filled with stunted trees. High up in a rock some several hundred metres away could be seen the weathered frescoes at the entrance to a cave. The year before from the mouth of this cave a ladder had hung sideways. Now it was gone. There had to be a story to that. Birds sailed around way below on thermals, or flew in and out of their own holes in the rock. Birds I could understand, but hermits isolating themselves in such unnatural conditions baffled me.

A written account in a biography of Athanasius describes how, during all night vigils of the great feasts of the Church, he would '...stand firm and erect like a statue; though sometimes in the detachment of his spirit and from his overwhelming love of God, he would become as it were deranged, rolling his head from side to side like one demented, and forget the part assigned to him in the service.' And yet people didn't see him as peculiar, they were filled with admiration. What was I to make of it all? Why did I try to make anything of it? Was I wrong to think him odd? Or were those who admired him right?

"Well?" said the Stoic, dismissing any further religious thoughts for the time being. "Do we press on? What other wonders do you have in store for me?"

We visited two other monasteries which required hips in good working order to scramble down narrow tracks and up a hundred steps. We reached the Barlaam Monastery. It was there that Robert Curzon had arrived in the nineteenth century having crossed the Pindus range with a party of 'friendly brigands' to guide him. The only means at the time to draw the attention of the monks had been to fire a gun. The only way to the top had been by precarious ladders pinned to the rock-face, or by a net which was winched slowly up, twisting and turning with its victim in mid air.

We entered the Katholikon and admired its frescoes - yet another of the Day of Judgement depicting the fearful figures of men whose souls were being tussled over. Above hell-fire sat Christ in glory surrounded by his saints. Way below, a monster fish with open jaw and evil eye was ready to receive the sinners down a shute of fire. On the left of this scene was the gentle figure of the Virgin Mary, and on the right that of Christ again, one hand up in a gesture of blessing, and the other hand holding the Gospels. This was my first visit to Barlaam and, as I was still in poetic and artistic mood, I continued to accept the 'You have been warned' frescoes. I couldn't help but wonder, though, why those who painted frescoes seemed to see Christians so askew? Why did they give saints eyes like fish and over-elongated bodies which made them look as though they were being hauled by the neck up to heaven?

We were drawn by an elderly man to see a mural depicting the fate of Alexander the Great. The skeleton in its coffin was a timely reminder to mortals that to be pagan and to be called great was but a transitory glory - there was still time for those alive to rise above such a 'dust to dust' fate, and to achieve eternal life. The man gave this information in hushed tones, and smiled confidingly as he tried to convey to us the Christian message of humility.

"Not that I relish the idea of eternal life," said the Stoic, when we'd freed ourselves from him. "I think I'd rather settle for 'dust to dust'. The thought of life everlasting is just too much. One life on earth is good enough for me. Now where are we going?"

It was difficult to decide which monastery church was the most beautiful: the Barlaam with its imaginative fresco of a monster fish with open jaw and evil eye? Or the Roussanou (now a convent) raised high like a dovecote on its pedestal, with its spectacular frescoes in the narthex depicting life and death, with every small detail of martyrdom at the hands of Roman soldiers: martyrs being put to the sword, or torn apart by wild beasts; or stretched or crushed or stoned or beheaded with blood gushing from the neck as the head (encircled by its halo) was caught in a basket. There was a martyr having his legs broken, another hanging upside down held by his legs with a sword being driven through his ear; another tied to a wheel and being turned over spikes; one being dragged by the legs behind a galloping horse; and yet another having the top of his head sliced through by two men using a cross-cut saw. And still more martyrs were depicted in picturesque detail: one being targeted by flying arrows with an arrow already piercing his shoulder and neck; another having boiling oil poured down his throat; yet another with one leg chopped off and laid to one side, and the second about to be chopped; and one with only his torso left, his arms and legs sticking out of a basket like sticks of French bread; one haloed martyr being boiled to death in a cauldron, and yet another being eaten by wild beasts.

"All these martyrs with their haloes, my dear! It makes you wonder about man's bestiality, and the almost absurd fanaticism of those early Christians. You might say that to bring out the bestial in others in order that you yourself can fly up to heaven is almost a sin? I wonder."

We entered the main body of the church. Here all the martyrs were ascending to heaven where angels were weighing the sinners and the saints on scales, and an archangel with a long toasting-fork was keeping many little demons at bay who were doomed to slink off to everlasting despair. To the right of these sinners were animals of every sort, whilst in the domed roof, revealed by light slanting through narrow leaded paned windows, was the figure of Christ receiving the martyrs.

I went to ask the nun at the entrance to this church about the frescoes, but found her talking earnestly with a distressed young woman. I returned to the church to wait, and soon the young woman came in and knelt on the stone floor, prostrating herself and weeping and kissing the ground repeatedly.

I wondered what the poor woman had done. Was she a novice who couldn't stay the course? Had she confessed something shocking to her Spiritual Father and been severely reprimanded? Or had he, for that matter, confessed something to her? My mind was full of thoughts fit for the world but not for a convent. I was sorely aware of my own shortcomings and tendency to dramatize. Before the young woman had finished her prostrations and weepings, we quickly left.

When we returned to Agios Stephanos I asked if the icon room had been blessed. Yes, we could visit it, we were told. I tried not to swell with pride at the thought that it must be the will of God that we should; humility wasn't one of my strong points.

The young novice of the previous evening accompanied us to a large well-lit room. In neat rows on tables were many small pots of coloured pigment, jars of clean brushes, and icons in various stages of completion. Many of them had only the traced outline of faces or partly painted bodies. The work was painstakingly slow and demanding, we were told. No artist was let loose to improvise with her artistic talents; each icon had to be traced from an existing one; gold-leaf was applied to the background and pigments were mixed for the colours.

We were shown the icon she herself was working on. It was of Agios Charalambos to whom the Katholikon was dedicated. To us the icon looked perfectly accomplished. She told us, however, that she had to go over the beard again because it had not passed the scrutiny of the Abbess who frequently came to inspect the work in progress. She accepted the criticism without resentment. Everything must be done in order to attain final perfection.

We still hadn't seen the monastery's small Church of Agios Stephanos. It had been built in 1350 and its earliest frescoes had been done in 1501. It stood perched on the edge of the rock near the terrace where we had been the night before.

An elderly nun sat outside the church quietly reading aloud from an open Bible on her lap. She looked up as we approached, and seemed very ready to break off from her devotions to have a chat. She asked us about our families and our travels. Then she invited us to enter the church whilst she herself returned to her reading. We could hear the gentle murmur of her voice as we wandered around the small twelve by fifteen metre building.

The story of Agios Stephanos Protomartyr (St. Stephen the First Martyr) is told in the Acts of the Apostles. He was stoned to death and died praying for his enemies before he 'fell asleep'. It is said that this church was built on the spot where an anchorite had taken up residence on the rock.

The small church was exquisite with its carved and gilded ancient icons, and its iconostasis topped by a wrought and gilded crucifix. The muted light made the frescoes mysterious. There was yet another skeleton in its coffin, which I took to be Alexander the Great, with a sorrowing saint standing by grieving that this 'great' figure was reduced to mere bones.

Perched as it was on the edge of the rock-face overlooking Kalambaka, Agios Stephanos had been badly damaged in World War II when the Germans had believed the monks, who had then inhabited the place, were sheltering the resistance. The monks were finally driven out by the Communist uprising following the war. It wasn't until 1961 that nuns took over the monastery and repaired this church. Now it stands snugly on its rock, keeping its former destruction secret from those who do not enquire about its history. Only its outer wall overlooking the town still bears the scars from machine-gun bullets.

This small, reconstructed church confirmed my belief that human beings are constantly having to draw everything back from chaos. To get the energy to do this requires something other than self, something which many people would claim to be the Holy Spirit or the will of God; something certainly which drives the mind to have the will to do it.

We were advised to arrive early for the Vigil which was being held on the eve of Pentecost. It would start at eight and would continue till one or two in the morning, but we could leave when we liked, we were told.

"I'll stay the six hours if you want me to," said the Stoic, "though it's long past my bedtime and I may fall asleep."

One of our novices greeted us as we entered the church, and brought two chairs for us to sit on at the back. That was a relief as usually in Orthodox churches the faithful have to stand for long hours at a time. I could cope with standing for half an hour, but for any longer my mind was drawn from things holy to mind-boggling concern about back-ache or fainting.

We were taken to see the relics which were in embossed silver reliquaries and laid out on two tables in the nave. The chief relic was the skull of Agios Charalambos. This was exhibited in a glass box which stood on a carved wooden stand. We looked down on the skull, the top of which had a small piece missing. We were told that it was now always kept under glass because it had been vandalized by someone cutting out a piece to keep as a souvenir.

Behind this relic was an icon of the saint strung across with chains, watches and trinkets as votive offerings for the many miracles he'd performed. In the past Agios Charalambos had averted plague and pestilence, and had brought great prestige to the monastery.

Our novice said that any nun having her periods was not allowed to kiss the relics, and as this was the case with her that day she couldn't perform that ritual. I supposed it was an old taboo thing about impurities and all that. I made the sign of the cross the Orthodox way, hoping that by doing it I might at least neutralize any heathenish thoughts lurking in my head.

There were three other relics: a ring of John the Baptist, a piece of the Holy Cross and a foot of a woman martyr, Agia Marina. The Holy Cross, of course, was discovered by the Emperor Constantine's mother, Helena, who, despite over three hundred years having passed, had miraculously managed to identify the cross on which Jesus had been crucified. Pieces from it are to be found all over the Orthodox world and are greatly valued by whoever possesses them.

The foot of Agia Marina was not a beautiful thing and had a hole in it as though a stake had been driven through it. We were told to bend and smell the sweet aroma which exuded from it. I couldn't detect any smell, and supposed I just wasn't on a high enough spiritual level to be attuned to such marvels.

We took our seats at the back, and watched the comings and goings of the nuns as they prepared the church. Candles were lit behind the reliquaries which cast a glow over the silver; vases of white flowers were placed before the iconostasis. Soon a reading began from the Gospels - first a nun read on one side of the church, then one on the other side continued, each responding to the other.

The lights were switched on in the sanctuary so that the heavily carved iconostasis, which was perforated in many places, became mysteriously lit from behind. The wine-red glass, and silver icon lamps hanging before it, threw a gentle light on the rich patina of the wood.

The antiphonal chanting now began. I noticed that the novice we had walked with on our first evening was in the choir on the right. As the chanting progressed and night came on, the church grew more mysterious; only the light from the candles flickered and cast shadows.

I was beginning to wonder if this would go on without variation for another four hours, when a majestic entry was made by a priest of great stature who strode in from the narthex. His presence seemed to fill the church as he kissed the icons and the relics before entering the right-hand door of the iconostasis.

The soprano chanting continued until the central Royal Doors of the iconostasis opened, revealing the dominant figure of the priest standing before the altar. The choir ceased to chant as the priest began to intone powerfully in a resonant bass voice. Leaving the sanctuary, he passed slowly down the nave, and censed all present in the church, before returning to the sanctuary where he removed his head-dress with a flourish, which released his long hair gathered back from his face. His large imposing, charismatic figure, now perceived through a haze of incense, stood before the altar, arms outstretched. In contrast were the small dark figures of the nuns on either side of the church with their white faces and peaceful expressions.

In my own depraved way I thought the priest rather sexy, but quickly banished such ideas from my mind. The nuns were right when they said the devil was always tempting, always trying to infuse an inappropriate thought which might grow like a snowball. Certainly it required the Holy Spirit to come down in tongues of fire to melt away the snow-flakes of wicked imaginings.

So, during the Vigil that evening, the power of the eternal good was invoked; so the forces of evil were dispelled, as those who believed themselves to be chosen by God prayed for the world. Through worship they did everything in their power to draw events back from chaos, and uphold all that was good in a strong invisible net of prayer.

"Food for thought, dear," said the Stoic afterwards, when we'd returned to our room. "Quite an eye-opener into the spiritual world for me."

"The Orthodox services are much more spiritual than the Church of England," I said.

"I was thinking during the service how I could still depend on myself even if I granted that there might be something other than self to be called on," she continued.

"Of course!" I replied.

"Of course, dear? Such a positive statement from you is quite unexpected!"

"It's just the way that 'something out there' has been fashioned and brought into the human context that I find a problem," I replied.

"That's the rebel in you, dear. Well, I'm dog-tired. Nighty-night." And the Stoic rolled onto her side like a large beached whale, and was soon asleep whilst, no doubt, the nuns and the priest prayed on till the small hours, communing with deity for the salvation of souls.

Ever wary that during the hours of darkness I might become a prey to holy wills or devilish ones, I again took a sleeping pill. I wanted, I supposed, to remain as long as possible a free spirit.

The following day we both bought an icon from the convent shop. When we came to say good-bye to the Abbess, we offered her a sum of money for our two nights under her care. Her gentle face expressed dismay at such financial gain but, when I said it was for the convent or for charity, her small white hand emerged from the wide black sleeve, and the money disappeared with the hand back into the folds of her garment.

A taxi was called to return us to the real world which somehow seemed light-years away. The taxi driver showed a certain deference towards us when he picked us up with our baggage from the entrance to the monastery.

As the taxi wound its way down to Kalambaka -

As we turned for the last time to catch a fleeting glimpse of the rock monasteries -

As our journey took us back to the noise and hubbub of everyday life -

I toyed with the thought that there had to be some prime mover other than self which had caused me to try to gain entry to the Agios Stephanos monastery. There had to be something which had first activated my enthusiasm and set me off. The will of God, if will of God it had been, was something that just couldn't be explained.

But later, when the bus bowled along taking us back to Salonika, and we passed the distant looming mass of Mt. Olympus on our left, I thought again of the old gods. The chameleon in me began to fade from the Christian holy to the other holy.

I was, in fact, quite pleased not to have been pulled

down the plug-hole of true Christian belief, as I was still free to plod on with the pilgrimage of searching. Perhaps that was the will of God?

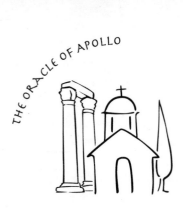

7

DELPHI

It was evening by the time we'd changed buses and were on our way to Delphi. We had come from Volos, the port for the northern Sporadic islands from which, for Harry's enjoyment, we'd taken a ferry to Skopelos where we'd spent three days.

We were now subjected to an exhibition of all that was most daring and heroic in the Greek spirit, as our macho driver with a black walrus moustache took to the mountains bearing us with him. The conductor quickly took our tickets, had a fag and a spit out of the window, then seated himself beside the driver and shut his eyes.

The scenery was spectacular. At one moment we were able to look down to the flat terrain below, with its mapped out shore-line, and the next we were being swung around another hairpin bend and the view was gone as we hurtled along the flank of the mountain towards the setting sun. The sky and clouds seemed to be on fire above the darkening barren mountain, until another hairpin bend was taken and we sped in the opposite direction along the twilit mountainside.

Harry sat bolt upright, gripping the seat in front with both hands. His knuckles showed white, and his eyes skimmed like tennis-balls backwards and forwards as we flashed past objects - long-horned cattle - sheep shacks - a whitewashed chapel - a peasant on a mule - a wayside shrine -

"I suppose you've taken out insurance?" Harry asked.

"Yes, of course! Though where the papers are I've no idea."

"What does it cover?"

"Loss of limbs - sight - up to a million pounds, I think."

"A million pounds?" Harry took his eyes off the road, and turned to make sure he'd heard correctly.

"Maybe two million. But you have to lose a limb, or be killed or something."

"Hum." Harry's momentary thoughts of easy money vanished.

It was nearly dark, and for some reason the driver thought it unnecessary to turn on headlights. I wondered if he had any, so dark was it, so fast were we going. We could see other cars who beamed their imminent approach, but they couldn't see us as we hurtled along down the middle of the road, overtaking several articulated lorries grinding their way downhill in low gear.

At last he noticed night had fallen and turned on his headlights; at last the on-coming traffic could see us. The conductor now opened his eyes and began to chain-smoke. Soon we saw the lights of Amfissa from where we had to take a taxi on to Delphi. At last we felt secure as, after a nightmare, you wake up screaming but find that after all you're still safe and well in bed.

"We don't have to do anything today, do we?" asked Harry hopefully. "It's nice just sitting here." It was early morning and we were on the terrace of our pension seated under a trellis of black grapes. From there we were able to look south to the distant Gulf of Corinth, and back up to the lower slopes of Mt. Parnassos and the Delphic oracle. Unidentified birds sailed on thermals way below us. It was tempting to sit and laze all day. Three or four other guests were also seated there drinking coffee and relaxing.

I had Homer's Hymn to Apollo on my lap, and was reading how Apollo had first founded his sanctuary at Delphi. According to the story, merchants (some say pirates) had been on their way to Pylos from Crete in a black-prowed galley when Apollo, disguised as a dolphin, leapt out of the sea and landed on the deck. This had been regarded as 'a portent great and terrible'. Apollo had then used his immortal powers to guide the galley towards the coast near to this sacred site and then, 'like a star at high noon, while the gledes of fire flew from him', soared from the boat to the heavens and descended like a meteor to his sanctuary. The people there had been amazed and fearful. Apollo had next appeared as a man, and had told these merchants/pirates that he had selected them to be his priests.

"Isn't it odd," I said to Harry, "that according to Homer's Hymn to Apollo, when Apollo chose his priests, he said they were to forsake their wives and families?" And I tapped the open book.

"Odd? Why odd?" asked Harry.

"Well, because Jesus said much the same thing when he chose his disciples centuries later."

"At least Jesus didn't turn into a dolphin," Harry remarked.

There was a curious link also - maybe a far-fetched one - between the dolphin becoming equated with Apollo, and the fish becoming the secret symbol of the early Christians. But then, if I wanted to be far-fetched, there was the star of Bethlehem which matched Apollo as a meteor marking his sanctuary site.

Apollo too was believed to be a god of peace, who tried to bring reconciliation amongst people. After killing the Python he'd taken himself north to the Vale of Tempe where he'd purified himself in the river Peneus. We had seen the area briefly from a bus - a beauty spot where the Peneus flows through the gorge separating Mt. Olympus from Mt. Ossa. After purifying himself, Apollo had then served as slave and shepherd to Admetus, king of Pherai in Thessaly, in order to atone for the killing of the Python. It was odd that sheep came into the Apollo story, and in the nativity account in St. Luke's Gospel there were also shepherds watching over their flocks.

It was even odder that Christ said he was the 'Light of the world', and Apollo had often been referred to as Phoebos Apollo (Apollo the shining one) and at one time had been equated with the sun and, therefore, the light of the world.

We gave ourselves a little longer before going up to the main sanctuary site. Once inside the gates we followed the ancient Sacred Way, passing the many Treasury Houses which were now mostly stone foundations. Apparently, there had once been monuments lining the route, gifts given to the sanctuary by the city states, the islands and newly founded colonies. Each had been presented in gratitude to Apollo for his guidance, each vying with the other in splendour and in value. Only the Treasury House of Athens, desiged as a miniature temple, stood undamaged and supreme.

Before any enquiry could be made of the oracle, it had been necessary for the priest to see that the day was suitable for a consultation. This had been determined by a sacrificial goat brought to Apollo's innermost sanctuary where it was sprinkled with cold water. If the goat began to tremble then the enquiry could proceed, if it didn't then that was the end of it for that day. The custom of using a goat was because it had been believed the cavity, the sacred source of oracular inspiration, had first been discovered by a goat.

The formality of any consultation had always been observed with dignity and ceremony, and I could well imagine the awe and wonder of coming as an enquirer to these foothills of Mt. Parnassos some two thousand years ago.

We walked up further and came to the Omphalos. Legend had it that Zeus had once let off two eagles from the far points of the heavens, and where they'd met had been pronounced the centre of the world - 'omphalos' is Greek for 'navel'. It was shaped like a giant egg but with a flat top where two gilded eagles had once stood. Its base was also flat. It had originally stood in the innermost sanctuary of Apollo's temple.

It was to this Omphalos that Orestes (son of Agamemnon) had come, pursued by the Furies (winged women who harassed those who were guilty of murder). He beseeched Apollo to give him relief from his tormentors, and was advised by the oracle to seek the wisdom of Athena.

The fifth century dramatist, Aeschyllus, described the

Furies in The Eumenides as being:

> '...dark of hue
> And altogether hideous, breathing out
> Their snorting breath in gusts not to be borne,
> Distilling from their eyelids drops of hate...'

"Cor, strike me if that's not the Omphalos!" A man speaking English was approaching from behind.

"Looks like a big stone to me," came a woman's voice.

"I've told you about the Omphalos. It's the belly-button of the world, it is!"

I was curious but didn't want to get involved. We walked on as the man was saying: "So this is where the lad Orestes came with all them Furies cos 'e'd killed 'is Mum, cos she'd killed 'is Dad - well, that's Greek tragedy for you, know what I mean?"

We came to the Sacred Fountain at the centre of the Sanctuary of Gaea, goddess of the earth, ('gaea' means 'earth'). The waters of this fountain had, apparently, been guarded by the monster Python/dragon.

"You know how the laurel or bay tree came about?" I asked Harry.

"Haven't the foggiest," came the reply.

I told him how the goddess of the earth, Gaea, had had a daughter, a beautiful nymph called Daphne, with whom Apollo had fallen hopelessly in love.

"They were always falling hopelessly in love," said the dismisser of romantic stories.

I ignored the remark, and told him how, in order to defend her daughter from Apollo's advances, Gaea had turned the poor girl into a laurel which, from then on, had become sacred to Apollo.

"And that," I declared, "is possibly the reason why the Pythia chewed laurel leaves before delivering her oracular pronouncements; why only laurel or fir was used on the sacred hearth where the eternal fire burned; and why the winners at the Pythian Games were crowned with laurel."

I looked around at the various ruins. "Somewhere here," I went on, "they had a festival called the Septerion which was celebrated every eight years to commemorate the killing of the Python. The role of Apollo was always taken by a child who would go up some steps to a hut to shoot the dragon. The child would then act out Apollo going to atone for his sins. Isn't that interesting?"

"What is?"

"The atonement idea. Apollo was said to be a god of atonement, and Christ also."

"Hum."

We continued on up to the temple of Apollo. The scenery was wild with rocks and trees and chasms to the west, a wonderful back-drop to the temple. Now only the paved area and six Doric columns remained. Beyond them a few cypresses grew like sentinels, their dark green a contrast against the deep blue of the sky. In its heyday, after being rebuilt because of earthquake, the temple had had six columns at each end and fifteen along either side, with a marble roof and pediments. Its presence there must have been spectacular.

The oracle had been functioning from the eleventh century B.C. By the sixth century it was wielding such power that no cult or institution could be changed or introduced without consulting the oracle first. Enquiries were also made concerning tactics in war and major political problems. Everything depended on Apollo's priestess (the Pythia) sitting on a tripod over the chasm discovered by the goat. From it vapour rose causing her to fall into a trance and become inspired.

Although the Pythian responses had often been in riddles and somewhat peculiar, they were sometimes astonishingly lofty and poetic. When Athens was in danger from the Persians, the Pythia's advice to the envoys who'd been sent from Athens to the oracle, had been to flee from the advancing enemy: 'Miserable men, why are you sitting idle? Leave in flight the furthest dwellings of your land and the high peaks of the wheel-shaped town. For neither head nor body remains firm, nor tipmost toes nor hands; nor is anything of the middle left, but it is reduced to oblivion...' The envoys hadn't dared return to Athens with this gloomy answer, so they went back for a second consultation. On this occasion Apollo had responded with a grain of optimism wrapped up in a riddle: '...yet Zeus of the broad heaven gives to the Tritoborn a wooden wall, alone to remain undestroyed, and it will bless you and your children...'

A wooden wall? The envoys had felt brave enough to deliver this conundrum from Delphi, and the elders of the city had scratched their heads, some thinking the wooden wall must be the wooden palisade around the Acropolis, and others that it was the Athenian fleet at sea. The latter had proved to be correct as, soon afterwards, there'd been the famous Athenian victory over the Persian fleet at Salamis.

Because of its extraordinary power and influence, opportunists had inevitably used the oracle for their own personal ambitions and political propaganda. But on the whole, whenever such attempts at hoodwinking had been tried, the offenders had been found out and severely punished.

I tried to imagine the interior of the temple - the cella, which would have been at the east end with the adyton, or inner sanctuary beyond. The eternal fire on the sacred hearth of Hestia had been somewhere there. Also the gold cult statue of Apollo together with the Omphalos.

The adyton, the most sacred part of the temple, was believed to have had a few steps down to the chasm over which the Pythia sat on her tripod. Some said that the bones and teeth of the Python had been kept in the bowl of the tripod

We heard the man speaking English approaching again. " ...then climbs onto 'er tripod what's over a sort of 'ole in the ground and up come vapours what make 'er inspired!"

"Sounds daft to me."

"Course it's daft, but it's what them did in them days. It's no more daft than some of them things you gets today. Now you gets the vicar in 'is pulpit talking 'is inspired words believing 'e's God's chosen. Now it's the congregation what falls into a trance. It's all daft!"

This time I turned and saw a bright-eyed British character in his late fifties wearing shorts, trainers and a T-shirt with 'Tower of London' printed on it. The woman with him was well built and taller than the man, and had an expression of patient resignation.

He must have overheard us talking in English as he spoke to us without hesitation. "Morning! Been 'ere in Delphi long?" he enquired conversationally.

"Since yesterday," I replied.

"Always wanted to come to Delphi," said the man. "I've read all about Delphi, I 'ave. If I was to go in for Master Mind I'd 'ave Delphi as me specialist subject, I would!" He addressed Harry: "I expects you knows all about Delphi.

You looks the sort what knows everything."

Harry said something to the effect that he only tagged along, and I was the one who was interested.

"That's like Elsie 'ere. She only tags along." He stood facing the temple braced and admiring, filling his lungs with air. "So this is it! This is what I've been waiting for!" I was about to say something but the man said: "Tell you what - whoever it was what came to consult Apollo, 'e 'ad to think pure thoughts and speak well-omened words. 'E couldn't come before Apollo griping about nothing. 'E 'ad to be in a state of purity, know what I mean?"

"Wouldn't suit you, then, would it!" said the woman.

"Nothing that the Castalian Spring couldn't purify!" came the instant response. And the man looked at us with brows raised and bottom jaw drawn back, defying us to disbelieve him. But he didn't wait for us to speak, before he was away again with the next thought.

" 'Twere Plutarch - Ploootarch! Funny name that! - 'Twere Ploootarch what was a priest 'ere, who said the interior of Apollo's temple were filled with a sweet aroma like a lady's perfume."

"With all them sheep and sacrifice and whatnot, I'd say your Plutarch weren't smelling anything of the sort," retorted the woman.

We smiled and nodded at them and, as we moved on, we overheard the man say: "Don't know what they did with the offal. Nothing I likes more than liver and onion - "

The scenery around was wild and rugged and we were soon beside the roped off theatre in honour of Dionysos, god of wine and drama. To be seated in this theatre watching some poetic and lofty tragedy by one of the great dramatists must have been memorable, situated as it was in this terrain.

Some legends claimed that Apollo hadn't killed the Python but had killed Dionysos who'd already been in possession of the sanctuary. Being immortal, however, he couldn't stay dead but always returned for three months during the winter – a resurrection of sorts. During these three months Apollo absented himself and oracular enquiries stopped.

We were about to move on when the British couple trudged up. "Dedicated to Dionysos, this was," said the man. "God of wine, 'e were. God of beer, if I 'ad me way."

I wanted to make some suitable comment but the man beat me to it. "Cor! Imagine sitting 'ere on a summer's night with all them 'ills and mountains all around. Better than the Apollo theatre in London, know what I mean?" Another thought like a meteor dived into his mind. "Tell you what – I wouldn't mind building a nice little bungalow up 'ere," he said with gusto. "Nice little 'oliday 'ome we could 'ave 'ere."

I noticed the woman pondering the matter before saying: "I'd 'ave me kitchen looking that way." She pointed to the view of trees and wild, rugged landscape. "Wouldn't mind washing me dishes looking out there."

We left them ruminating happily and continued on up to the stadium above.

The Pythian Games had at first been held every eight years to commemorate Apollo's eight years in the Vale of Tempe. From the sixth century they were held every four years and included such events as boxing, wrestling, athletics and foot-races, as well as music and poetry contests and drama in the theatre of Dionysos.

Sitting on one of the top tiers beside the stadium, we watched a group of young French students running races. The remains of the entrance through which the athletes had once passed were still in place and, at the starting line were marble slabs set into the ground with holes in them for posts to separate the athletes, and grooves in which to place their feet when crouching ready to sprint off.

We saw the man and his wife arrive at the stadium, and heard the man say: "I expects they 'ad chariot races. Cor! I'd like to've seen them chariots doing their Grand Prix! I expects they turned over!"

In no time the man had found the marble slabs at the starting line and was trying out sprinting postures, turning his body this way and that, to see which would give him the best advantage to get off to a good start in a race. The woman sat watching.

The man said: "Now I've run me race we can go down again! Upsydaisy!" He held a hand out to the woman.

"I'm not going nowhere. We've only just got 'ere!" she objected.

"Please yerself," said the man, and seated himself beside her.

We came down from our higher seats and passed by them, nodding greetings and farewells. I said that we'd no doubt meet again somewhere in the sanctuary.

As we were crossing the stadium to leave, I overheard the man say: "Wouldn't mind a nice little 'oliday 'ome up 'ere neither! Don't know if they'd 'ave water 'ere, mind."

"Better enquire of Apollo, then," said the woman.

Back down by the Treasury Houses we stood beside a group gathered before large blocks of stone. Their tour guide was telling them that those with crosses on them had been brought to the sanctuary by Constantine, the first emperor to accept Christianity. She went on to announce that he'd also removed pagan works of art from the sanctuary to adorn his new city of Constantinople.

It was Constantine who was said to have seen a shining cross in the sky before the battle of the Milvian Bridge with the words 'by this sign conquer'. The sign ('labarum' as it was called) was, in fact, already a symbol embroidered on the Roman cavalry standard. All that was needed to Christianize it had been to add the Greek letters 'Chi' and 'Rho', the monogram of Christ. Particularly interesting to me was the fact that originally it had been an ancient symbol of Hlios (the sun), not forgetting that Apollo had once been equated with the sun.

Although Constantine had accepted Christianity as a true religion, he hadn't been so Christian that he'd been prepared to turn his back on his old pagan favourites such as Apollo, Zeus and Athena.

Apollo himself had been approached and questioned regarding Jesus. Apollo had responded that Christ was a wise man who'd worked miracles and had died a 'bitter death'; he had then added that the miscreants were the Christians who insisted on worshipping his mortal body when it had been torn and disfigured by nails. The Christian cult was absurd, Apollo had said, and God incarnate was a myth.

"Well, Apollo would say that," said Harry glibly when I informed him of these weighty matters. And I went on to tell him how Caesar Augustus, soon after the birth of Christ, had either come himself or sent an envoy to the oracle concerning his successor. The response from the Pythia had been: 'A Hebrew boy, a god who rules among the blessed, bids me leave this house and go back to Hades. So go in silence from my altars.'

The last oracular pronouncement from Apollo's Pythia had been delivered to Julian the Apostate (brought up a Christian but wanting to turn back to paganism). The response had been: 'Tell the King, the fairwrought hall has fallen to the ground, no longer has Phoebos a hut, nor a prophetic laurel, nor a spring that speaks. The water of speech even is quenched.'

"Well, if it only spoke in riddles, much better to be silent!" said Harry positively in response to this bit of information. "Paganism!" he scoffed.

We went on down to the lower terrace to see the three columns which still remained of the temple of Athena Pronaos. This would have been the first temple to be reached for those arriving from Athens or from the port of Itea along the Pleistos valley, now a dry river-bed filled with silver-leafed olive trees. At that time the Delphic site with its columned temples, marble edifices and back-drop of mountains, would have been dramatic and totally awe-inspiring for those arriving by sea to seek advice from the oracle.

On the same terrace as the temple of Athena Pronaos was the excavated outline of the gymnasium. This had been the training area for athletes preparing for the Pythian Games.

A Byzantine monastery, the Convent of the Panagia (All Holy) had once stood there, built on the site of this gymnasium. In 1898, however, it had been demolished in order to expose the ancient site again. It struck me as weird that it had been thought appropriate to destroy the Christian presence in order to reveal the pagan past. But in the nineteenth century there had awakened such interest in antiquity that it had been thought right to do this. The village of Kastri, which had sprung up over the ancient Delphic site, had consequently been demolished, and the villagers rehoused in what is today's town of Delphi.

As we stood alone by the site of the old gymnasium

with the temple of Athena Pronaos nearby, I thought up a little story about how the pagan gods had finally in their own way triumphed because they'd found the one chink in contemporary Christian armour - money. That men might thrive let Christians reveal the pagan past which drew the tourists and brought revenue. The pagan gods are laughing!

On our way back we came to the Castalian spring which was situated at the base of the towering Phaedriades rocks near the main sanctuary site. The Phaedriades rocks were twin crags from which water issued down a narrow gash. The area was pleasantly cool and shady under lofty plane trees. The water cascaded into a paved area where purification had once taken place before any enquiry of the oracle could be undertaken. As noticeable also, however, was the British couple, the man with his arm hooked through the woman's. He was staring upwards with a look of wonder on his rugged features.

They turned as they heard us approach, and the man immediately waved a wet hand at us and declared himself purified. Then he said: "Complete submersion for anyone what done a murder." Then he added: "That lad Orestes done a murder - that's why 'e were 'aunted by them Furies. Wonder if 'e 'ad complete submersion before making 'is enquiry of Apollo?" This was followed immediately by: "Wonder if them Furies 'ad complete submersion with 'im?"

Once more we smiled and nodded our farewells, and left them at the Castalian spring. We walked back towards the museum.

Outside it we stopped beside an ancient floor mosaic depicting geometric patterns and figures within medallions. It had been part of a fifth century church dedicated to St.

George. I was interested in the name George because as far as I could make out it had never been used before the Christian era. It had formerly been an epithet of Zeus (Zeus Georgios - Zeus, protector of the earth). In Greek the word 'earth' is 'gaea' and the word 'georgio' is a compound of 'gaea' (earth) and 'ergein' (to work).

It seemed to me that the George and dragon legend echoed the story of Apollo killing the Python/dragon.

We'd attended an annual three-day festival of St. George at the nearby village of Aráchova a few years earlier, in which the killing of a local dragon was celebrated. The village had a church dedicated to St. George, and inside it a column had been pointed out to me believed to have been part of an old temple of Apollo.*

We were about to turn away when we heard the familiar voice approaching. "...if I were a pirate and then found I were a priest serving Apollo - well, I don't know 'ow I'd feel about it!"

"Do you good, Sam!"

"You'd like to be married to a priest, would yer?"

"I'd rather be married to a pirate!"

"With a parrot on me shoulder and skull and cross-bones on me cap?..."

Their voices faded as they headed for the town and disappeared behind the line of tourist coaches drawn up beside the road.

As we returned to our pension a black cloud like thick black smoke swept up the valley and engulfed us. It was as if Apollo was behind and, with a big puff, was blowing the cloud on towards us.

That night the weather was wild. Our pension seemed to take the full force of the gale as window-shutters creaked and banged, and the wind howled and the rain battered.

* For details of the festival see Chapter 9 of the first Ye Gods!

Perched as we were on the edge of the valley we seemed to be the punch-ball for all the elements coming in to the attack. We shivered and shook through the night like the goat brought before Apollo's altar, whose visible trembling revealed whether the day was auspicious for an enquiry.

The following morning the weather was calm and warm again, though there was a definite feel of autumn in the air and there was snow on Mt. Parnassos. We sat out on our terrace under the trellis of black hanging grapes, whilst our landlady hung her sheets out on a clothes-line set up to one side. I felt at any moment our tranquility might be broken and we'd hear the cockney couple coming down the steps from the road above. But nobody disturbed us.

It seemed amazing that life went on as usual never mind what happened; never mind how wild the weather; never mind how much one speculated on paganism or Christianity. Ask a thousand questions, debunk a hundred pagan myths or Christian stories, and the Corinthian Gulf was still there, a vivid blue against the mushroom grey of the Peloponnese beyond; still the olive groves remained as grey-green and silver spectacles of quiet reliability, with here and there a cypress rising tall and slender from them. House martins still flew about as did small fly-sized insects which were flitting restlessly with whirring wings catching the sunlight in sparkling bursts of rainbow colours. Such things were comforting when probing the immortal world; comforting because they never changed from being positive realities.

CHAPTER

8

OLYMPIA

I told the receptionist we were going on up to the mountain village of Andritsina before continuing to Olympia.

"Andritsina?" she queried, and there was a hesitation in her voice and a darting look in her eye.

"What's it like?" I asked.

Pause. Shrug. Then she said: "It's different. The mountains are beautiful but the people, they are - " and she shrugged again before adding, "they are political."

"Political?" asked Harry. "Ask her what she means."

The receptionist who'd heard him, answered: "In the war the people they are communist; they fight up in the mountains. But now there is no problem," she added reassuringly.

I tried to encourage Harry: "If it's political you'll find it really interesting," I said.

"I don't want to stay amongst communists," Harry objected.

"There are hotels. Look! It's a really nice mountain

village with a large plateia surrounded by plane trees and pastry shops," I said. And I showed him the evidence of a well written brochure which he didn't look at. "You see? It caters for tourists. And the temple at Bassae nearby is unbelievably spectacular!" I actually had the write-ups muddled but, as Harry didn't read it, he never noticed my mistake.

As the one and only daily bus to Andritsina had long gone we had to take a taxi. The driver spoke the most incomprehensible Greek I'd ever heard so we drove in silence for the fifteen miles, except for Harry making grumbling comments as he sat on the edge of his seat scanning the wild terrain for bandits. "Why go to some ruin in the back of beyond, when there are dozens of ruins in more civilized places - just because some idiot wrote about it - no one else here on the road - typical brigand country - "

We first saw Andritsina from the distance; it looked picturesque with its houses tucked into the mountainside. As we approached we noticed graffiti scrawled across the road and on the walls of some of the houses: ELAS - KKE. ELAS was the communist dominated Greek resistance movement in World War II, and KKE the Communist Party.

I wanted to ask the driver about it but we were totally incommunicado regarding such things. I asked for the plateia and in a moment he'd drawn up in the road beside what looked like a junk-yard filled with crates of empty bottles.

I repeated the word 'plateia' and the driver grunted and pointed to where we were. There were a couple of plane trees but certainly no pastry shops. I asked him to drive on, and in a moment we were out of the village again.

"Andritsina?" I asked. He replied with a bad-tempered shrug.

I asked for a hotel and the driver turned about and put us down outside a large featureless building.

"We're not staying here!" said Harry.

"Is there another hotel?" I asked.

The driver took this as a personal attack and inexplicably yelled several incomprehensible sentences. He couldn't have done a better job of getting Harry out of the taxi.

We made our way into the large, empty hotel. There was no one at reception and, after pressing a bell a number of times, a woman eventually came shuffling down from the W.C. whose flushing could be heard. That at least meant there was water and plumbing.

There was an air of desertion about the place; an air of take it or leave it irritation at anybody coming at all. Staff enthusiasm didn't exist, and toleration of guests (of us only it seemed) was barely disguised fury. We asked if they served supper. This was met with a blank stare, a shrug and some mutterings about spaghetti.

After a great deal of fumbling with a key in a faulty lock, we eventually got into our room which, in fact, turned out to be quite nice with a balcony overlooking the road.

When we'd unpacked we went out to explore. We saw another building with the word 'hotel' on it but it had dilapidated balconies and broken window-panes. I tried to cheer Harry up by commenting how much better off we were with the hotel we had. Only the thought of the great temple of Apollo at Bassae kept up its beckoning finger.

We entered the village's small museum whose exhibits looked like an array of household objects laid out in a car-boot sale. A woman attendant sat knitting in a corner. When we'd completed the circuit I asked her about a library of rare books which I'd read the village had, but she knew nothing of it. We were then directed to a small shack to find out the times of buses for Olympia the next day.

Inside this dark hole of a place a hoary-faced, elderly man sprang up from behind a counter. He grabbed us by the hands and shook them effusively. Then, with garlic-laden breath and through rotten teeth, he informed us in broken English that he loved Jesus, and we were his brother and his sister. After some time of persistently shaking our hands, and expounding on the joys of being a true Christian, he finally gave us the bus times which revealed to Harry the bad news that there was only one bus daily, and it left at eight-thirty in the morning. This put us in a quandary. Harry wanted to get on it and I wasn't going to miss seeing the temple I had come up for.

"I tell you what," I said reasonably, "you go down to Olympia, and I'll see this blessed temple and join you later by taxi."

This received the expected answer: "What? And leave you alone up here amongst these crazy people? No, no, we'll stay together."

"All right," I answered, "I'll make you a promise. If it's so excruciatingly awful at the hotel, then we'll take a taxi down to Olympia after doing the temple." To which Harry snorted something about wicked expense just for a ridiculous temple.

To soothe his jangled nerves I told him about the beauty of its structure; how its architect had been the man responsible for the Parthenon, and how the marbles from this temple were now in the British Museum. This promptly brought the retort that if they were there, then why the hell were we here? To which I could only answer that since we were here, it was unreasonable to suggest I should be there.

When we got back to our hotel we found things livening up. A wiry, grey-haired bunch of middle-aged American cyclists were bicycling up the mountain road in pairs and dismounting at our hotel. There were many scribbled notes on the reception desk informing the cyclists where each was sleeping. One note said that they were to dine at a taverna beside a plane tree in the plateia. One weather-beaten American woman looked woebegone because 'Madame' (as she called the bored-out-of-her-mind receptionist) had blown her 'taap', the reason being that she'd unwittingly banged her bedroom door and the plaster on the ceiling had come down.

As we sat down for supper that night there was a power cut. It was not unexpected because a number of wild-cat strikes had been called by disgruntled workers, something which we ourselves had been warned about but to which 'Madame' it appeared had given no thought. It resulted in a lot of scurrying around by the glimmering light of a fast fading torch. She never ceased to have a resigned, bored expression as she reluctantly produced candles wedged with crumpled paper into empty wine bottles.

Supper was a tepid slab of spaghetti with some old grated cheese sprinkled over it. No pudding. Our candle burned out before we'd finished the meal, and a fresh stump was brought which just saw us up to our room before that too expired. Candles had been planted at strategic places up the stone steps, their light casting eerie shadows along the dark, wide corridor. It seemed that the hotel staff had no sense of fire hazard as many candles leaned precariously at angles, one of which I extinguished as it was so close to a stack of canvas chairs they were becoming scorched. I wondered if they were deliberately trying to burn the place down.

Our thoughts that night were of fire and murder. Monstrous shadows were thrown by the guttering candles on the stone stairway; a lighted profile seen one moment, then darkness as the profile and candle vanished around a corner.

We sat out on our balcony by a dwindling candle-stump and ate grapes. It was a fine, clear night and the cicadas were noisy in the dark. Occasionally there was a tinkling of bells from distant sheep. After a while the cyclists returned from their taverna two by two, carrying their cycle lamps.

"I bet they'll all be ill before the night's out," Harry remarked.

I called down to one of them. "Did you have a good meal?" I asked.

"Goat," came the reply. "They called it goat."

"They called it goat!" scoffed Harry. "Oooof! it's just what you'd expect in a place like this!"

The following morning Harry found a dead beetle on his plate under his table napkin. On the plus side, however, two of the American cyclists told us they had a minibus which normally carried their luggage, but which in half an hour would be taking them to the temple of Apollo, and we were welcome to join them. By now Harry was resigned to the fact that some things had to be tolerated in the pursuit of art.

"Any of you guys know something about this temple?" enquired a friendly American woman in dark glasses and a navy baseball cap as we set off on the trip.

"You'd better ask my wife," Harry said. He seemed relaxed and I supposed it was because he was amongst fellow English speaking beings.

I told them how the temple had been built in honour of Apollo who'd delivered the nearby Phigalians (whoever they were) from the plague. Another possible theory was that the temple had been built up in this wild terrain because the Phigalians had fled up to the mountains when their village (wherever that was) had been attacked. To build a temple in honour of Apollo was their way of giving thanks to the god for his help and protection.

"So what century would that be?" asked a man.

"The fifth century."

"And would that be B.C.?" he enquired mildly.

"That's a goddam silly question, Chuck!"

"Well, how would I know, honey? It's way before my time."

"You know who put it there?" asked a woman.

"The architect Ictinus, the same man who built the Parthenon," I replied.

"The same one who built the Parthenon, guys!"

"Wow!"

"All the way out here, so far from habitation!"

"Apollo's temples tended to be in wild mountainous landscapes," I said. And I told them how an unusual feature of the temple had been that, instead of a cult statue, Apollo had been represented by a single short Corinthian column standing in solitary state to the forefront of the cella. Two ideas put forward regarding this unusual feature were that it either represented the tree of life, or was symbolic of the palm tree clung to by Apollo's mother when giving birth to him. An opening to the east of the temple had allowed the early morning sunlight to flood into the cella, illuminating this solitary column as well as the line of taller columns the length of the temple, imparting mystical light and shadow throughout the whole building.

"Wow! You don't say! Columns of mystical light!"

By now we were all leaning forward, searching the landscape for the temple, each eager to be the first to spot it.

We arrived.

"What in the name of Gaad!"

All eyes stared in dismay from the minibus window. Instead of the temple standing supreme against the skyline we saw a giant canvas.

Amidst expletives of disappointment, we descended from the minibus and found we had to buy tickets to go inside. But the magic of the place was altogether gone. Without the landscape there was no way that the ancient monument could be appreciated. The shock of it left me stunned as we wandered gloomily amongst the many columns within the confines of this canvas covering. We were to learn later that UNESCO experts had made a study of the temple and had found considerable deterioration due to water penetration of the limestone. When this froze in winter it caused cracks resulting in more damage. The columns had now been treated, and it was imperative to protect them for the time being from extreme weather conditions. I made a mental note to return one day to see the temple unwrapped and standing supreme again in its natural surroundings.

"I knew it was a gross waste of money coming to Andritsina!" Harry proclaimed with convenient hindsight when we were heading down to Olympia by taxi - the bus services had gone on strike. And I rather agreed with him.

"Well, if we take our bearings from the W.C. up here," said Harry pointing to the site-plan, "you can see we're going south, so this presumably is the Gymnasium."

Harry was showing a lively interest in Olympia and on this occasion it was I who was honour-bound to keep up with him. Tall pine trees offered comforting shade to beleaguered tourists.

The tour guides marched past with their charges, and glanced at us with contempt as we twisted the site-plan this way and that to make sense of it. Only by joining their classical tours and paying for their expertise could we hope to wander intelligently amongst these marble ruins. Good heavens! What else could we expect but to feel bemused when the whole site had been ravaged by two huge earthquakes in the sixth century A.D.? It had then lain dormant for centuries to come, under layers of silt washed down by the two nearby rivers, the Alpheus and the Kladeos. Years of painstaking excavations in the nineteenth century had finally brought the ruins to light again.

There was no sign of the two rivers, though a recent aerial photograph revealed a broad winding river nearby. In ancient times the Alpheus had been navigable, and part of the Olympic spectacle had been the state barges bringing V.I.P.s to the games. Visitors had also sailed in by sea from Piraeus or from outlying colonies. Otherwise the crowds had come overland down the Peloponnese.

There were several legends regarding the origins of the games. Some said they were much older than the first official Olympiad held 776 B.C., and had been first founded by Hercules after he'd completed his sixth labour of cleaning out King Augeas' stables. King Augeas reigned in Elis, and Hercules had rather sensibly made the labour easy for himself by deflecting the river Alpheus, so letting its waters wash away the piles of dung for him - something no farmer could do in Britain today without incurring the wrath of the River Board Authority and a crippling fine.

Yet another legend claimed that the site had been chosen by Zeus himself who'd hurled a thunderbolt from his throne on Mt. Olympus.

A third legend was about a man named Pelops. As an infant, Pelops had been killed by his father who'd wickedly served him up in a dish to the gods to see if they could detect any difference between human and animal flesh - though how this story came about is difficult to understand, as the immortal gods are known to eat nothing but ambrosia. Only Demeter had eaten a portion of his shoulder because she'd temporarily lost her wits whilst grieving over the abduction of her beloved daughter. The other gods, however, weren't fooled, and they miraculously brought Pelops back to life, and restored his shoulder by replacing it with an ivory one.

When he grew to manhood, Pelops heard that the local king was offering his daughter as bride to any man able to out-distance him in a chariot race. Whoever failed was killed, and his head mounted on the palace walls. There'd already been twelve suitors who'd suffered this fate. Full of confidence, Pelops presented himself at court but, having no intention of losing his head, he sensibly used it instead to hatch a cunning plot. He discovered that the king's charioteer was also in love with Hippodameia (the king's daughter), and so promised him a night with her if he saw to it that the wheels of the king's chariot fell off during the race. This the charioteer fixed, but when Pelops won the race and, therefore, his bride, he shabbily failed to fulfil his side of the bargain, and murdered both the king and the charioteer.

"That wasn't very nice," remarked Harry in a supreme understatement.

We came to the foundations of the Prytaneion, the administration centre for the games. After reading the information on it from our booklet, Harry informed me that the building had had in it the Sacred Hearth of Hestia on which the holy fire had burned continuously. It was from this flame at Olympia that all sacrificial fires had been lit on the altars of the gods, or was taken for the founding of a new colony.

"Hestia? Never heard of her. Who is she?" Harry demanded.

"She was the sister of Zeus, and goddess of the hearth and family," I said. "In fact, households honoured her then just as in Greece today they honour the Virgin Mary in their homes, and light candles before her icon."

We went on to the next ruin. "Bouleuterion," Harry announced. After consulting the booklet, he added: "It was here that everyone came to swear an oath before a statue of Zoos that they wouldn't cheat or bribe and would observe all the rules of the games." He strode around the ruins whilst I sat down on a column drum. It was a change to see Harry getting involved in a site. "Do you want to go down there?" he asked, pointing southward to a row of broken columns.

I felt I could see as much as I needed from where I sat. "You go and I'll wait here." I took the booklet and saw that he was now going to the Southern Colonnade, a place where anyone with something to hold forth about had held forth. At the height of its fame Olympia had been the location not only for athletes, but it had also been a public platform for rhetoricians and poets; a market-place for merchants and artisans; a showground for the rich to parade themselves, and for politicians and writers to be heard, knowing that their ideas and writings would come to the attention of the greatest gathering of people come from all parts of Hellas.

Before every Olympiad a sacred truce was called during which time no one was allowed to take up arms, or continue legal disputes; thus everyone attending the games was guaranteed a safe passage. Initially the sacred truce had been for one month but in time had been extended to three months.

It seemed an excellent idea. Why, I wondered, had the custom ever been abolished?

I noticed that we'd missed the workshop of Phidias on which an early fifth century church had been built. When Harry returned we retraced our steps.

Phidias had been responsible in Athens for the cult figure of the goddess Athena and the Parthenon marbles. Here he had created the cult statue of Zeus which had been pronounced one of the seven wonders of the world.

Where his workshop had been the remains of the early Christian basilica could be seen. There was a lattice-work stone screen containing within it Greek Orthodox crosses, with a central gap in it to the sanctuary where the altar would have been. I noticed that from that point the Christian altar would have had a perfect alignment with the temple of Zeus whose steps ascended to the temple from the east. The gold and ivory cult statue of the god would have faced east towards the rising sun, something the Christian Church had adopted, not as I'd always supposed, in order to face east because Christ was born in the east, but because the rising sun, the new dawn, the new 'light of the world' was symbolic of Christian hope.

We left the workshop and went on to the temple of Zeus, a massive area of paving blocks and column drums. Harry took the booklet from me and thumbed through it as we stood on the hefty paving slabs. He found an illustration of what the cult figure of Zeus would have looked like.

Suddenly he said: "Why has Zoos got an angel perched on his hand?"

"An angel?" I looked at the picture. "That's no angel, that's a Nike."

"A Nike? What's a Nike?"

"It's symbolic of Victory," I said.

It was an easy mistake to make, and I reminded him of the statue of the Roman emperor we'd seen in the Archaeological Museum in Salonika, whose armour had had on it figures with huge deep wings crowning him emperor. With the coming of Christianity many artists had depicted angels as winged Nike figures so that pagans would equate Christianity with Victory.

We walked to the west end of the temple where the cult statue of Zeus would have been looking eastward.

"The interesting thing about the cult figure of Zeus is that Phidias created him as a god of love," I told Harry. "He completely broke with the Homeric tradition of Zeus, the thunderer, who wreaked revenge on those who angered him, and instead turned him into a sort of God of the New Testament full of fatherly concern. A number of people, both pagan and Christian, remarked on his new expression of divine love. Don't you think that's interesting? I mean, interesting that the idea was beginning to seep into the human mind five hundred years B.C.?" I asked.

"Hm, maybe."

"Stand here - just exactly here," I instructed. "You have

to imagine the grand procession coming to this temple on the last day." And I told him how on that day a procession consisting of the judges, the administrators, the priests and the victors had come to stand before the god. The winners of each event wore filets of wool around their heads, and carried a palm branch in their right hand. It was there that they were finally crowned, standing before the great statue of Zeus. It wasn't until the winner's name was called out by the herald that he received his wreath of wild olive - unlike athletes at Delphi who were crowned with laurel.

"Like standing on the podium today with the National Anthem playing, I suppose?" Harry suggested.

"Except that in the early days it was a sort of communion with the supreme god, and an acknowledgement that the winner had received divine favour and patronage," I said. "I think that rather nice."

A party of portly Germans temporarily blocked our view as they followed their guide to the east of us. They waddled past in white cotton sun-hats with cameras slung around their necks.

Harry began reading from the booklet. "This says the temple had marble roof-tiles," he remarked. "Imagine a marble roof with the sun shining on it!" He skipped through, muttering sentences before announcing: "And on the east pediment there were marble sculptures depicting the story of Pelops colluding with the charioteer before his chariot race, with the centrally placed taller figure of old Zoos. Hum. Presumably approving the cheating and murdering that took place so that Pelops could win his Hippo woman."

Harry, with one eye on the site-plan, began looking for the now no longer extant altar of Zeus. The altar had been built where the thunderbolt was believed to have struck the ground, hurled by Zeus from his throne on Mt. Olympus.

The altar was thought to have existed as early as the tenth century B.C., and was originally a small and simple affair. Eventually it had become an important landmark with a perimeter base of a hundred and twenty-five feet, with ramps giving access to a platform up which the sacrificial cattle could be driven. The ash from previous sacrifices was never removed, and so it grew until it was as high as twenty-two feet, requiring steps to be cut into the compressed and hardened ash-mound in order to give the priest access to the top.

It was customary for the great sacrifice to take place on the third day of the games. A solemn procession came from the Prytaneion, and a hundred bullocks were slaughtered on the lower platform, their carcasses cut up and the legs carried up the steps to the top where they were burned in honour of Zeus. The rest of the meat was used for the Ritual Banquet held in the Prytaneion on the last evening of the games.

"The Ritual Banquet was a sort of communion between men and deity," I said. "It was believed that Zeus was present at the banquet."

"Umm. Well, people will believe anything, I suppose," Harry remarked.

"Yes, they will," I agreed, ready to argue over what people believed today. But Harry was in no mood to debate such matters, and I contented myself with only saying: "If you're looking for the old altar you won't find it because the Christians destroyed it."

The Olympic Games had continued to flourish until 391 A.D. when all pagan cults had been banned by the Emperor Theodosius I. Some records show that the games had ended then, being regarded as anti-Christian; others that the last festival had been held in 425 A.D., after which Theodosius II had ordered the destruction of all pagan temples. As for Phidias' chryselephantine statue of Zeus, it had been transported to Constantinople where it had remained until destroyed by fire.

We went on to the Heraion. This temple of Hera was much smaller than the temple of Zeus and was, in fact, a much earlier construction built in the seventh century B.C. Before his own temple had been built two hundred years later, Zeus had shared the Heraion with his wife. According to legend Hippodameia - the ill-gotten bride of Pelops - built the Heraion in gratitude to Hera (goddess of marriage) for the unexpected gift of her cheat of a bridegroom.

"You know who was the offspring of that marriage?" I quizzed Harry.

"Not a clue," came the answer.

"Atreus, king of Mycenae." Pause. "Father of King Agamemnon," I explained. Pause. "The Trojan War Agamemnon," I said.

"Oh, him! Married to Kilem-something."

The party of Germans kept dogging our footsteps. There was also a group of Japanese who were chattering to each other and looking fresh as daisies in the afternoon sun. We saw the Germans turn in a troope and waddle away, their knees sagging with exhaustion. The bright-eyed bunch of Japanese, with their raven black hair and dark glasses, turned en masse and followed the delicate lotus bloom of their tour guide, going in search of what? Yet another colonnade? Or, perhaps, the site of the Hippodrome which had been washed away by the flooding of the river Alpheus? It hardly mattered that nothing remained of it because the mind's eye was quite capable of visualizing the chariots; the stamping of impatient horses, the holding of these steeds, the starting signal, and away with them all in a cloud of dust.

We went up a grassy embankment to the terrace where small elegant buildings, many looking like miniature temples, stood in a row.

"Treasury Houses," said Harry, "where money and gifts were deposited."

Apparently, each had been built by some distant city state or Greek colony, and had served as a sort of club-house, a convenient meeting place for those who had come from afar. It was possible, from the vantage point of the grassy terrace on which the Treasuries stood, to watch many of the events.

Harry, having taken his earlier bearings from the W.C., decided it was where he needed to go next, so he disappeared whilst I walked down to the Stadium on a lower level to the east. Rather suprisingly it didn't seem to be part of the 'classical tour' itinerary, and I was quite alone there. It had been constructed around 350 B.C. outside the Sacred Grove where once the earlier races had been held. One of the myths regarding its six hundred foot length was that Hercules had run the distance in one breath.

Amazing! To one side of the Stadium was the Judges' Stand where I was able to sit in glorious isolation and look both ways along the track. A gently sloping man-made embankment had enabled as many as forty-five thousand spectators to watch the events.

I was more interested in the small marble Altar of Demeter Chamyne opposite the Judges' Stand. There the priestess of Demeter had once sat enthroned; she'd been the only woman allowed to watch the races. A strict rule had existed that no married woman was permitted to come to the Olympic Games on penalty of death. On all other occasions, however, women were allowed into the sacred precincts.

I wondered why there had been this honour allowed to the priestess of Demeter. The priestess had to be married and was chosen from a noble family for each Olympiad. I imagined it had been an honour shown to Demeter because the goddess had been the only one of the Olympians to have been tricked by the dish containing human flesh. It was, perhaps, a way of appeasing the goddess for the evil done her on that occasion.

I sat on silently with a vision of antiquity passing before my mind's eye. To my left beyond the Stadium there was a vaulted tunnel from which the judges and athletes had entered the Stadium. It was the oldest known tunnelled structure (thirty-two feet long) from the classical Greek period, with its entrance in the Altis (the Sacred Grove). It had a bronze trellis-gate which was opened at the beginning of the races allowing only those eligible, such as the judges and the athletes, to enter. It must have been a spectacular moment for those waiting around the Stadium, when those taking part first emerged from it, comparable to the cheering crowds when football teams march out into a stadium today.

I examined the booklet and discovered the events for the five days listed. There'd been boys' races, wrestling and boxing contests on the first day after the initial swearing-in ceremony in the Bouleuterion. On day two, chariot and horse races had been held in the morning, and in the afternoon the pentathlon which consisted of throwing the discus, the javelin, jumping, running and wrestling. On day three, after the morning procession of judges, ambassadors and competitors, and after the official sacrifice of one hundred oxen at the great Altar of Zeus in the morning, there'd followed foot-races in the afternoon. Day four had consisted of wrestling, boxing and the penkatrion which was a fight to get the opponent to the ground and never mind the means. This had been followed in the afternoon by a race in full armour which must have demanded stamina, as the games had been held in mid-summer and the heat must have been intense. Then, on day five, there'd been the final procession to the temple of Zeus where the names of the victors had been called out, and they'd been crowned with their wreaths of wild olive in the presence of the great cult figure of Zeus. The day had ended with feasting and general celebrations.

I looked across at the tree covered Hill of Kronos. Kronos had been the father of Zeus, his mother being Rhea. The Hill of Kronos had in the earliest days been an oracular seat where those who had the ability gave predictions by listening to the birds. They also read omens by examining the way the hides of the sacrificed cattle burned.

By now the sun was in the west, and its late afternoon light was casting long shadows towards the east. I liked the idea of lighting the Olympic flame here from the sun, before relaying it around the world to the host nation holding the games, an ancient tradition from the great orb and light of the world since the first Olympiad. I supposed that without this extraordinary 'light' humanity wouldn't exist, which was a humbling thought.

I saw Harry waving at me from the Treasury Houses, and said a silent farewell to the solitary peace of the Stadium. "Time for the museum now!" announced Harry when I joined him.

"Oh." Energy and momentum had to be kept up,

though I would have preferred to have had another day for it. But as usual, there were dead-lines to be met, and other places to see before our flight home.

At the museum we saw the metopes from the temple of Zeus depicting the labours of Hercules, the interpretation of which by both pagans and Christians was the necessity for man to overcome the evils of the world. We admired the beautiful clay figure of Zeus abducting the child Gannymede, which act of homosexual love could only have added fuel to the fire of Christian antagonism towards pagan god morality. We looked at the weights held by the athletes in order to give them the impetus for a long jump; and we saw the finds from the workshop of Phidias which included his own mug, on the base of which was inscribed in Greek 'I belong to Phidias'.

By the time we'd finished with the museum we were drained of the last drop of human energy. We dragged ourselves back to our hotel for a well earned rest, limp and sagging at the knees like the troupe of Germans we'd seen at the temple of Zeus.

"Come on over, join the gang!" We were standing out in the road reading a menu which was attached to the wall of a picturesque taverna which had lanterns hanging from the branches of plane trees. Seated at a line of tables were the American cyclists; two of them were half out of their seats as they waved us over.

They made a space at their table which was stacked with crockery and half empty platters. They'd been having an early supper in readiness for a dawn start next day. What was to be a quiet evening for us became filled with

American voices and cycling chatter. Unexpectedly the subject came around to bicycling in England.

"Hey! I've a wild idea! Let's plan our next trip! How about we make it England, guys?"

I saw Harry flinch.

"We can head west to Harry's homestead."

"England? I like the idea!"

"Am I right in thinking your Cheddar cheese comes from down your way?"

"And is it there they make cider?"

"Hey! Plymouth is south-west, maybe we can look up our forbears! How about that, folks?"

"Is it where you go fox-hunting on horses?"

"Where you live, is that where they have hedgerows?" asked one.

"Hedgerows? Well, yes. Very high hedges and banks and narrow lanes. Quite dangerous for cycling."

"Hedgerows! By that do you mean rows of hedges?" asked another.

"And hills," said Harry. "Very steep hills."

"Boy! After these mountain passes your hills will be nothing to us, honey!"

"And we can stay nights in your English pubs! And look in on you folk!"

"Hey, guys! That's settled then. Next stop England!"

A toast was drunk and with many slaps on the back, and assurances that Harry could expect them in the early summer, they finally departed. Suddenly the taverna seemed silent and deserted. We were left to ourselves.

"Why did you encourage them?" Harry demanded

"I didn't. You were the one being nice."

"All of them! Why didn't you mention rain? You could have discouraged them with the weather."

"Well, why didn't you?"

"A whole bunch of wet cyclists!"

"We could arrange to be away."

"Away?"

"We could plan another trip to Greece in early June," I said. It was the perfect moment for suggesting such a thing. But I didn't pursue the subject, knowing it was best to let Harry think about the pros and cons for a while.

I studied the menu and noticed there was grilled 'lamp chop'. The last time I'd had 'lamp chop' I'd supposed it to be a misprint for lamb, but had found it nothing like lamb and indescribably tough. When the waiter came I questioned him closely.

"Nai, nai, lamp," he assured me, ('nai' means 'yes' in Greek). Knowing that it was perfectly acceptable in Greece to be shown the food before ordering it, I asked if I could take a look. With the customary little nod, and the gesture of the hand to follow him, I was taken to the back of the restaurant where the weighty door of a cold store was opened to display all the cuts of meat inside. He showed me the 'lamp chop' and I could see at a glance that it wasn't lamb - small donkey, perhaps, or large goat, but not lamb. Near to it I saw a side of beef hanging from a hook and felt beef would be appropriate to the occasion - like at the Ritual Banquet at the end of the ancient festival. We ordered two grilled steaks.

Sitting out under a plane tree by lantern light and enjoying our meal, I could imagine Zeus looking down on us two mortals eating filet steaks, as once he had on the celebrants of old.

"Why did they only sacrifice the legs to old Zoos?" demanded Harry, helping himself to more salad. "Surely it was a bit of an insult, and they should have sacrificed the rump or topside, or at least the best cuts of meat?"

"It was a sort of double-think idea," I replied. "The Greeks knew the god could only eat ambrosia, so they sacrificed what they didn't want and had a good banquet themselves. It was often the only time people ate meat. A bumper occasion. In fact, it was remarked on by Tertullian, an early Church Father." And I told Harry how Tertullian had wagged a finger at pagans, declaring that he didn't blame them at all for sacrificing the worst parts to the gods. In fact, he thought it showed remarkable wisdom on their part, as they clearly knew that otherwise the meat would be entirely wasted.

"Sometimes," I remarked, "it's a great advantage being human, don't you think?"

"Well, certainly I wouldn't want to be a god and faced with just a hoof," came the satisfied reply.

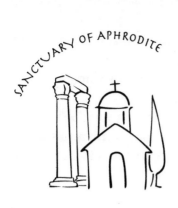
SANCTUARY OF APHRODITE

CHAPTER

9

CORINTH

"I will ask the boss," said the long-haired beauty at reception. "He will enquire for you. He is not here now but will come later."

The Boss when we met him was an old man in his mid-seventies with a round, beaming, slightly grizzled face. He wore an ill-fitting suit and a brown felt hat turned up all around. He was anxious to please and, on hearing our request regarding public transport for a day trip to the town of Kalavrita in the mountains, he disappeared into his office and began telephoning about the time of trains before making further enquiries regarding buses.

"Did I hear you say Kalavrita?" enquired an elegantly attired woman. I had noticed her reading a 'Hello' magazine and glancing at us occasionally over it. She was subtly made up, was past middle-age and had a lively eye.

"I've heard of Kalavrita. Where is it?" she asked.

I told her it was in the mountains and could be reached by rack-and-pinion railway up a gorge.

"What an adventure! How fascinating! I've only just

arrived in Corinth and haven't yet made plans. I suppose one must see the old part?"

"We're about to go there," I said, wishing immediately that I hadn't.

"I might come with you, that is if you don't mind. I'm no bother. It's just easier as a lone woman to travel with others." She tossed her short, curly blonde locks defiantly, a gesture made quite frequently.

Emerging from his office at last the Boss gave us a piece of paper with the information written on it, and asked us pleasantly where we were from.

"From England," I replied, hoping that it was a good country to be from. His face, which had had a cautious but polite expression lit up, and I swelled with pride. Had we been from Germany it might well have been different, because in World War II all male inhabitants of Kalavrita over the age of fifteen had been massacred; the town clock had stopped for good at the hour the slaughter had taken place.

"It is very good England," he said, and shook hands with us. The woman, whom we later referred to as the 'desirable lady seeking companion', declared she'd lived in England all her adult life but was born and educated in Ireland.

I hadn't expected the Boss to go to such lengths regarding transport to Kalavrita. It wasn't even certain that we would go to the place, it had only been an idea if we had the time. In fact, as it turned out, we never did get there; at that precise moment our immediate thoughts were fixed on Corinth and its environs.

On the bus to old Corinth we repeatedly saw in the distance Acrocorinth, the solitary upheaval of rock rising from the flat landscape. On its summit there had once stood a small but important temple of Aphrodite, goddess of love, patroness of all aspects of love, lust and erotica. The Desirable was seated in the bus in front of us, but had turned sideways in her seat to talk to us - well, to Harry who was seated on the outside.

"It was so interesting! I made my own arrangements but I was lucky because I had a friend who had a contact, and he arranged for a guide."

She was speaking about a trip she'd made to the Himalayas where she'd trekked, no doubt very elegantly, around the foot-hills. "You should do it," she said to Harry. "I've names and addresses."

But Harry responded in the only way he knew: "Couldn't possibly afford it," he said.

"Oh, it wasn't at all expensive. To do it in a tour would be quite dreadful. I doubt if the whole trip cost more than a thousand. I'm not rich, you know. I was lucky and had an aunt who left me a little. Tell me about your travels."

"We don't travel much - just around Greece. My wife's keen on old sanctuary sites and Byzantine churches," Harry said.

"Oh, so am I! So fascinating! Have you been to Russia? I spent a month travelling by train - " And she entertained us with her anecdotes and adventures, and the people in high places she knew, adding in all her lovers for good measure. "I'm the first to admit I make a rotten wife, but a very good lover - I don't like the word mistress, it's so aggressive."

I tried to keep my mind on our impending visit to Corinth but found it difficult. I was aware that her elegant laced up shoe had a life of its own, and each time the Desirable tossed her locks her shoe edged closer to Harry's hiking sandal.

In the first century Corinth had been a busy international port, a cosmopolitan centre, where merchants and seafarers sailing in from west and east would have seen Aphrodite's temple and thought 'aha!' As Corinth had been regarded as a centre for sexual pleasure St. Paul, who had lived there on and off for two years from around 50 A.D., must have been regarded as a complete prude preaching as he did about the love of Christ, the love of God, sexual abstinence and morality. At that precise moment I was all for St. Paul.

"So tell me more! Where do you hide yourselves when you're not travelling around Greece?" But, before either of us could answer, a good-looking man seated across from her intervened, having overheard her speaking about Russia.

"Excuse me - " he began. "You speak about Russia? Please - always I want to visit the places you speak of."

"My dear man, who are you?" asked Desirable with an air of never speaking to strangers.

The young man presented her with a card, and Desirable's eyes widened. "A German psychologist? And so young?"

"I am not so young," said the German smiling.

She immediately turned her attention on him, and began talking about her adventures in the Black Forest. The German had done a lot of walking in those parts and had studied for a while at Heidelberg University. As a psychologist he greatly excited Desirable who implored him to psycho-analyse her as she was so complex she couldn't understand herself.

Soon her attention strayed, and she began glancing at the countryside. "I've no idea where we are. Have you? Do you know what that mound is over there?" She was pointing to Acrocorinth. The German told her how it had been a centre of sex and love under Aphrodite, to which she reverted to her Irish roots and replied: "Jesus! The nuns wouldn't have liked that! I was brought up in Ireland, you know." She began talking about her Roman Catholic upbringing and how she'd been cured for good of religion by her convent education. "Can you believe it, I knew nothing about sex before I was married? Can you imagine that? Straight out of a convent with 'him'!" Her nose wrinkled cheerfully as she tossed her curly blonde locks tantalisingly. "Oh, have we arrived?" Her eyes scanned the buildings of old Corinth as the bus slowed down and came to a stop. The German psychologist got up. He was very tall and very polite, and stooped in order not to hit his head as he waited for us to pass. Desirable put a hand to his arm and said: "How tall you are!"

"It is two metres I am," said the German.

"And your mother managed to produce you?" asked Desirable with mock amazement.

"And my father too," said the German with smiling solemnity.

We left Desirable with her German who was a ready captive, and made our way to the ancient site.

It was midday and the sun was hot, though a slight breeze cooled us. We went first to the temple of Apollo and wandered amongst the seven fluted Doric columns which were all that remained of it.

Was it coincidence that, according to tradition, the first bishop of Corinth had been named Apollos? And was it coincidence also that the first church founded by St. Paul at the eastern port of Corinth, had a deaconess named Phoebe, a female version of Phoebos which itself had been a well-known epithet of Apollo - Phoebos Apollo, meaning the bright, the shining one? Could it be that these early Christians had been baptized into the Christian faith and given the name or epithet of the old god to blur the edges between paganism and Christianity?

From where we stood we could see Desirable and the German walking past the ruins. Neither of them appeared interested in the temple or the nearby Fountain of Glauke, a monolithic rock with two cave-like entrances into whose waters Glauke, the unfortunate bride of Jason (Jason of the golden fleece) had leapt when she'd caught alight by spontaneous combustion as soon as she'd donned a poisoned garment sent to her by Medea, who was a wild jealous woman and Jason's first wife.

When Desirable and the German were gone we moved on to the ruins of the Fountain of Peirene, an ornate series of arches over dark chambers with some decorative pillars. From the furthest chamber water flowed over large stones before being channelled away. It was a surprisingly peaceful and shady spot where it was tempting to sit indefinitely and listen to the cooling sound of rippling water. It was known as the Fountain of Peirene because a girl of that name had howled and wept so much at the death of her son that she turned into this permanent flow of water. Peirene had been the daughter of a river god, and Poseidon had been the father of the son who'd died. Harry's reaction when I told him was that it couldn't be too difficult for the wretched girl, since she was the daughter of a river god, to turn into a spring.

According to legend also, the winged horse Pegasus, born from the blood of Medusa, had drunk from this spring, and Bellerophon (a hero similar to Hercules, though less well known) had caught Pegasus at this spot and used the horse's magic powers to aid him with several labours that had been assigned to him. Pegasus was a favourite of the Muses and became symbolic of flights of the imagination.

We left the Fountain of Peirene and lost ourselves for a while in the Agora. We could see Desirable and her German walking towards the museum. We found ourselves near to a group whose tour leader was a nubile young woman with long dark hair, and wearing a navy baseball cap. She looked foreign but spoke good English as she held forth about old Corinth, telling her audience how the Agora had been not so much a market as a place full of workshops supplying the needs of the sanctuary.

When she and her party moved on, we mounted the Bema, a platform paved with marble slabs. From there St. Paul had addressed the crowds.

Words. The ability to communicate. Words, I told Harry, had seemed to take on a momentum of their own after St. Paul; they'd appeared to come alive and had started to propagate themselves in the strangest manner, claiming to be the one and only truth.

"But suppose all those words were playing about with men and, instead of the truth, they were spreading a great big lie?" I queried.

Harry merely said that if I couldn't believe in the truth of Christianity then it was better to keep quiet and stop voicing my opinions. But I found it difficult to remain silent when I had one.

At the far end of the Bema was a large block incised with the words in Greek and English from 2 Corinthians 4:17. They were fairly illegible with many letters worn away. I managed to make out the English: 'For this slight momentary affliction is preparing for us an eternal weight of glory beyond all comparison...'

Out came an opinion: "You've only to promise the

poverty-stricken riches in heaven, or the depressed eternal bliss, and whether it's true or not you're bound to get converts," I remarked.

"And why not? Everyone needs hope," said Harry reasonably. "Without something to believe in you may as well shoot yourself."

"People don't shoot themselves just because they don't believe," I objected. "I don't want to shoot myself. People didn't kill themselves worshipping the old gods which the early Christians said were mere poetic fancies." But Harry preferred not to think too much about Christianity, accepting it for what it was in its finished state, and never at all as to how it came about.

We decided we had time to see Acrocorinth if we took a taxi to it. As we approached a nearby taxi rank, we caught sight of Desirable sitting at a taverna with the German. She waved and called cheerfully to us: "Come and save me from this dreadful man!" We had no intention of saving her, and didn't think she had any wish to be saved either. We told her we were going on to Acrocorinth. "Oh, how interesting. How do you get there?" When we told her by taxi to the base, and then there was a steep climb up it, she said: "Dear God, have we the energy?" And she put an arm with its many fine gold bracelets out to the German.

He smiled patiently. "After the rest if you wish we will go," to which Desirable tossed her locks and said: "The goddess of love? How can we resist!"

Our taxi wound its way up the hill, and put us down at the base of Acrocorinth where the great defence walls coiled around it. We walked up a stone path which led through the first of three massive medieval arched entranceways.

St. Paul must have pursed his lips with disapproval at the ancient customs of this city, all under the guidance and patronage of a pagan goddess who was a delusion, and whose legendary goings-on left a great deal to be desired. What sin! What immorality!

Aphrodite had had her own colourful love-life. Married to the lame god Hephaestus she'd had an adultrous affair with Ares, god of war. Hephaestus learned about this, and cunningly created a gold net which was so fine it was invisible. When he knew his wife and Ares were having it off together, he threw this gold net over them and trapped them in each other's arms. He then called his Olympian relatives to witness his wife's adultery, and they all laughed aloud at the two caught up together. What an indignity! Ares, god of war, and Aphrodite, goddess of love, two contrasts yet uniting oddly and understandably; the one of love highlighting the other of war. Did St. Paul, who'd been brought up a Jew and educated in ancient Jewish traditions, know about Aphrodite's legendary love-affairs?

Unlike paganism, where people moved freely from god to god and there was no compulsion, Christianity had high expectations and disciplines. St. Paul set standards, and converts were expected to toe the line to apostolic authority. The Christian dogmas had to be accepted and taken on trust. Ask no questions - believe the unbelieveable - become a Christian or be damned.

I thought how it was all very well for St. Paul who'd had a blinding light conversion from which his Jewish past had burst into its new Christian state; he couldn't help but believe. But why, I wondered, if God had enlightened Paul and was said to be Almighty, didn't he enlighten everyone?

We paused by the arrow slits in the massive stone defence walls. Through them the advancing enemy would have been spotted in the plain below, or sailing in by sea. It was amazing how wide an area could be viewed through them. We walked on up and came to a small church dedicated to St. George, the warrior saint, a very suitable dedication where unseen martial powers needed to be harnessed for defence purposes. We passed a small mosque where Moslems had once found their consolation and hope as they'd called on Allah's protection. On up and up and up. We were glad of the bottled water we'd brought with us as we sweated our way onwards and upwards.

In its heyday the temple was said to have had no less than one thousand prostitutes to entertain the mariners and merchants who visited the city. In fact, the word courtesan is more appropriate for these servers of the goddess; they were slaves selected for their beauty, and bought by those who had the money, to be presented to Aphrodite in grateful thanks for some benefit received. One such example was an athlete who promised the goddess two hundred girls if he won at the Olympic Games. He did win and kept his vow. Some of the greatest sculptures of Aphrodite were, in fact, modelled from these Hetairai serving the goddess. Many of them were skilled in music and were there to entertain their clients.

I would have thought sex was the last thing people would have in mind after the hot sweat of the climb to the summit. We ourselves were merely pleased to have made it to the top at all. The views were magnificent with a cooling breeze which I supposed soon restored any beauty lost on the ascent.

With the coming of Christianity Aphrodite's temple was replaced by a church, and the sensual love of Aphrodite was substituted for the far more difficult-to-achieve love advocated by St. Paul. St. Paul's famous first epistle to the Corinthians had been written when he had been in

Ephesus. He had heard reports that his converts at Corinth had broken into factions, and far from loving each other were quarrelling amongst themselves. He was aghast at the way things were going, and was particularly shocked by the news that one of his converts had been having an affair with his stepmother. 'Shall I come to you with a rod, or with love in a spirit of gentleness?' he wrote. He was upset because it was against even pagan standards that a man should have it off with his father's wife.

I wondered what sort of letter St. Paul might write to Christians today, after two thousand years of warnings and sermons from pulpits. Or would he be pleasantly surprised that Christianity had spread, even though many modern bishops challenged the early Church dogmas? Was religion, in fact, coming full circle to a sort of pagan belief in unseen powers such as winged Pegasuses?

"Holy Mother of God! What can you think of me?" We heard the voice of Desirable, and a moment later we saw the German's head and shoulders and then the curly blonde locks of Desirable with a becoming straw hat, coming up towards us. "So help me God, I wasn't suggesting anything of the sort! Ah, I've found you both, thank the Lord for that! This man's been telling me the most terrible lies. Can you believe it? He says I'm beautiful and I'm a flirt. Dear God, he's been frightening me with the most terrible stories about Aphrodite. What was the last one? You tell the story while I sit down and get my breath back." Desirable found a rock and sat leaning back on her arms watching her new conquest.

"It is the young man Hippolytus - you have heard of Hippolytus?" the German asked. "He is the son of Theseus who is the king of Attica. Hippolytus, he loves the hunt and he worships the goddess Artemis who is the virgin.

And one day Hippolytus he says he scorns the goddess Aphrodite, he does not need the love, all he wants is the hunt. And Aphrodite she is very angry when she hears it, and she wants to punish this man. She makes Phaedra, who is the new wife of his father, to - how is it you say it?"

"To fall in love," said Desirable, leaning back on her arms and waving a leg in the air.

"That is correct. Phaedra she fall in love - "

"Falls, dear boy," cried Desirable.

"Ah, yes! She falls in love with Hippolytus. But, he does not falls - "

"Fall!" called Desirable.

"He does not fall in love with Phaedra. This makes her so very much unhappy - so very much angry - that she says to Theseus that Hippolytus he try to - "

"Tries to!"

"Yes, thank you. He tries to - how you say it?"

"Seduce! Rape!" cried Desirable.

"Ah, so. And she tells this to Theseus who is very angry. He asks Poseidon that he kill his son. It is a tragedy because Phaedra she kill - s herself, and Hippolytus he soon too is dead."

"So the moral to all that is - " Desirable patted the rock beside her, "never go to Greece where tragedy lies around every corner. Come and sit down, Helmut." She tossed her locks at him, and held out her hand. We left them sitting side by side.

On the bus back to Corinth Harry counted our money and found that we had very little to see us through the weekend. The banks were already shut and we needed cash. At our hotel we asked our long-haired beauty if they took travellers cheques but she shook her head. We should ask the Boss, she said, he'd know which hotel would do it.

As the Boss spoke no English, I said in Greek that we had a problem. He raised his grizzled head with its felt hat turned up all around, and his eyes widened with slight alarm. A problem? What was our problem, he enquired? No doubt he was expecting me to report a blocked drain, a smashed mirror or there was no water, or some other hotel maintenance difficulty. I told him that our problem was we'd run out of money and the banks were closed.

"That is no problem," said the Boss. "How much money do you want?" He took a bulging wallet from an inner pocket, and started counting notes out on the table as though we could have all the money we wanted. I settled for the equivalent of fifty pounds much to Harry's alarm, as he preferred to have the problem so there could be no expenditure.

I was delighted, and shook his hand and quite spontaneously kissed his grizzled cheek. He beamed with pleasure and said: "I keep it a secret from my wife! She will be very angry if I tell her I have been kissed by an English woman!"

Never had a financial embarrassment been so easily solved.

The following morning, using our new-found wealth, we took a taxi to Isthmia. It was there at the sanctuary of Poseidon that in antiquity crowds had gathered for the Isthmian Games, held every other year in the spring. Pausanias, the second century A.D. travel writer, described

Poseidon's sanctuary as he had seen it - a far cry from today's ruins: 'As you go into the sanctuary, there are portrait statues of athletes who won at the Isthmian Games, and some pine trees in a line, mostly growing straight up. The temple itself is no higher than the trees; there are bronze Tritons standing on it. In the front of the temple there are two Poseidons, an Amphitrite (Poseidon's wife), and a Sea, all bronze...'

The events themselves consisted of foot-races, boxing, wrestling, chariot races, and there had been competitions for musicians and poets. The winner of each contest was crowned with a wreath of wild celery, an award which didn't go unnoticed by St. Paul who, in his effort to reach out to the pagan mind, asked why an athlete would want to go to all the trouble of disciplining the body, when only one competitor could be the victor, in order to win only a 'perishable wreath'. Much better for all to discipline themselves for Christ as each would then gain a wreath which was 'imperishable'.

The sanctuary was far from being the splendid one described by Pausanias, but was a mass of tumbled column drums and ruined foundations. Only the Roman baths contained an exquisite floor mosaic depicting Nereids, octopuses and fish in a swift flowing movement.

From the sanctuary we could glimpse the sea. Money, now being no object, we took a taxi on to the ancient port of Kencherae in its horseshoe bay. It was where St. Paul was thought to have arrived by sea from Athens, and definitely the port from which he had departed for Ephesus. It was now no longer a port, though the ruins of its ancient quay and warehouses were still visible under the clear shallow waters along the shore. Here there had been an early Christian basilica church, and it was where the woman Phoebe had been deaconess.

Aphrodite, having first risen from the sea at Paphos in Cyprus, had become associated with the sea. She was petitioned by mariners as Aphrodite Pelagia (of the sea). They trusted her to bring them safely into harbour, thus enabling them to honour her in her other capacity as goddess of love.

Several early women martyrs had been named Pelagia, and all had been beautiful. Pelagia of Tarsus (St. Paul was from Tarsus) had been so beautiful that the Emperor Diocletian had wanted to marry her; but she'd held out against him, and had been roasted alive for her refusal. She'd met her death with courage, believing that to die in a swift roasting was a better option than being married to a pagan emperor and, as a consequence, roasting for eternity in hell.

The general opinion of scholars is that these martyred Pelagias were purely legendary figures with no historic foundation, and we shouldn't suppose they were anything to do with Aphrodite Pelagia. Why, I wondered, shouldn't we suppose it?

In her capacity as goddess of love, Aphrodite had covered the essence of love in all its aspects, something which pagan Greeks had considered natural to life and not a sin. That had come later with Christianity. The Church regarded love and sex as a moral danger to society, and homosexuality as a downright abomination. Gone were the days of joyful indulgence, instead came guilt and the fear of hell and damnation.

St. Paul (who had never married) wrote a whole chapter giving advice regarding sexual relations. In his first letter to the Corinthians he wrote: 'To the unmarried and the widows I say that it is well for them to remain single as I do. But if they cannot exercise self-control, they should marry. For it is better to marry than to be aflame with passion.' As if marriage solved all problems!

We walked the few metres that were left of the paved Sacred Way along which pilgrims would have come to the sanctuary of Poseidon at Isthmia. St. Paul would have taken this road. Maybe he would have turned to look beyond the bay to the distant mountains of Attica and Athens, whose inhabitants had proved such a stubbornly unresponsive lot when he had preached to them there. After Athens it was amazing that St. Paul still felt able to turn the minds of the Greeks from their perfectly happy state of serving the old gods. Yet against all the odds he succeeded, and the tide did turn, if very slowly, over the course of several centuries.

That evening we learned from the Boss that Desirable had checked out. He didn't elaborate on her departure except to say she had left in the company of a tall young man - a German, he believed. The Boss appeared indifferent as he shuffled papers together, but I wondered what went on behind the closed shutters of his face. Did he take an interest in the goings-on of his guests?

We went out and had supper at a taverna near the port. Afterwards, we walked along the quay beside which small boats and luxury yachts were moored. We sat on a seat and surveyed the scene. A container ship came sailing up the Corinthian Gulf and headed for the isthmus and the Corinth Canal.

"Here comes a tug!" Harry remarked, looking at the landmass through binoculars. The opening to the canal couldn't be seen from where we stood. "The canal has to be just there north of the white building," he went on. As I didn't know where north was, 'white building' was the only thing that meant anything to me.

The container ship stopped moving, and the tug too (now clearly visible) appeared also to be waiting. Eventually, after about ten minutes, a motor launch, which had obviously been blocking the passage through the canal, sailed out into the Corinthian Gulf. Soon the container ship was having two ropes attached to her, and like a proud outrider before a sleep-walking monarch, the small tug drew the ship forward. It wasn't long before the tug vanished, and the container ship's hull too gradually disappeared out of sight, leaving only the white bridge visible; then it also passed into the rising landmass as it was towed slowly forward through the narrow, sheer-sided man-made waterway to the Saronic Gulf.

A serious attempt to dig a canal, thus saving shipping a two-day sail around the Peloponnese, had first been considered and undertaken with enthusiasm by the Emperor Nero - he actually dug the first shovelful of earth with a golden spade. The enterprise, however, had come to nothing or rather had been halted because, according to one source, Nero's engineers had thought the waters of the gulf on one side higher than on the other, and the result might prove as catastrophic as the breaching of a dam. Many people were fearful also that Poseidon would be angry at the violation of his isthmus.

We strolled to the end of the quay, and watched the occupants of the yachts preparing their evening meal, or sitting on deck relaxing over drinks. The yachts were picturesque with their lights and their masts and rigging. We wandered back to the end of the harbour. The sun was setting and lights were coming on along the opposite shore of the Corinthian Gulf. On the extreme point was a lighthouse whose flashing light gave regular and frequent warnings to approaching shipping. It marked the rocky point near to which was an ancient Heraion we had once visited. The temple ruins nestled in a small cove, its tumbled grey columns and sacred altar in quiet solitude beside the turquoise sea.

The question I'd kept asking at the time was why had there been a temple of Hera built there beside the sea? Why a temple of the goddess of women and marriage in a cove, and not a temple of Poseidon, god of the sea? To me it had presented a great mystery.

Looking towards it now across the Gulf, the reason for it suddenly dawned on me. Hera and Aphrodite had been goddesses of two quite different aspects of human life, Hera of marriage and procreation, and Aphrodite of sexual pleasure. Could it be that the temple of Hera was there to warn all who were sailing to Corinth with the enjoyable intention of visiting the temple beauties of Aphrodite that, whilst they could indulge themselves for a while, they must not forget their responsibilities back home? Was it a cautionary reminder to every family man that he had a wife and children waiting for his return?

I realized now that to have a temple of Hera there visible to all passing ships, in fact made perfect sense.

CHAPTER

10

ATHENS

"So what's the plan for tomorrow?" Harry asked. It was the evening of October 3rd, the feast-day of St. Dionysios, patron saint of Athens. I was in bed with a bandaged hand, the result of being hit by a motorbike that afternoon. We had been to the Church of Agios Dionysios in Kolonaki, the smart residential area of Athens where, because of the feast-day of the saint, there'd been celebrations going on all day.

Whilst at the church I'd felt far from holy, and rather disappointed in the comparatively modern building. After the icon had been carried around the church, it had been placed centrally, and the pious had begun queueing up to honour it. I'd thought of joining them but had then felt it would be ridiculous for me to fake a devotion I didn't feel.

The accident had happened soon afterwards, and ever since I'd been trying not to regard it as divine retribution for not having honoured the saint. We'd been crossing the road between cars in a traffic jam, and I'd been holding my arm forward to let drivers know what we were doing, when suddenly my arm had been struck and I'd been whirled around to find myself looking into the startled face of a motorcyclist; I seemed to be gripping his handle-bars. The young man had at first been dumbfounded, but soon had shouted furiously as though it had been all my fault. I was so astonished I'd been quite unable to say a word before he'd readjusted his motorbike, and had roared off through the traffic, whereupon I'd yelled abuse after him.

A patch of blood had spread across my shirt, and my mind had raced in circles supposing I'd been stabbed through the heart, or had lost an arm or leg without realizing it. I'd checked myself out, and found a gash on the end of my thumb. Harry had been torn between behaving as though nothing had happened, and not looking over anxious about a conspicuously bloody wife. We'd found a chemist where an attentive assistant had patched me up. "How you do it?" he'd enquired. "Motorbike," I'd answered. "You ride motorbike?" I felt I was a disappointment when I'd told him I did no such thing.

Now, in answer to Harry's question, 'So what's the plan for tomorrow?' I said I'd like to go first to the Acropolis to pay my respects to the Parthenon, then to see the theatre and sanctuary of the god Dionysos, and afterwards to the Areópagus.

"Better see how you feel in the morning," Harry advised. "You may find you suffer from delayed shock."

"What happens with delayed shock?" I asked.

"You may not want to do anything." There was a note of optimism to his voice.

"Well, I feel all right so far," I said, swallowing a pain-killer when he wasn't looking. In fact, I thought I might have a torn muscle in my shoulder, but I preferred not to give Harry any encouragement on the 'doing nothing' idea.

I lay flat on my back, my hand with the bandaged thumb across my chest to my shoulder, like an effigy of a queen on a sarcophagus.

The following morning I felt remarkably well apart from a stiff shoulder. It was a fine, warm autumn day and the sky was blue with a few shreds of white cloud. A light breeze was refreshingly cool.

Whilst Harry strode around the Acropolis for exercise, I sat on a marble block near to the Parthenon whose marble columns and sculptured pediment exuded great holiness. It was extraordinary that, despite the loss of many of its marbles, it still had supreme majesty.

I could see no trace of its conversion to a church in the sixth century. Then it had been dedicated to Agia Sophia (Holy Wisdom), no doubt as a deliberate ploy to attract pagans who were used to coming to the Acropolis to honour Athena, goddess of wisdom.

The only justification for Lord Elgin removing the Parthenon marbles was that if he hadn't taken them for England, then the French would certainly have had them. But poor Elgin suffered as a consequence. It was almost as if all twelve of the Olympian gods had taken their revenge on him. The first calamity had come when the ship carrying them foundered off the coast of Greece, and the marbles had had to be salvaged from the sea bed at great expense to Elgin. Next, his wife (no doubt fed up to the teeth with marbles) had left him, taking her fortune with her. Then a son had died and the surviving one had epilepsy. Finally, Elgin himself suffered from an unfortunate disease which disfigured his nose and his career prospects vanished.

But, worst of all, the British Museum didn't at first want the wretched marbles so they lay around for years - not to mention the fact that some so-called connoisseur of antiquities suddenly declared them to be Roman copies, and not the Greek originals at all.

I left the Parthenon, found Harry, and together we walked down to the ancient sanctuary of Dionysos south-east of the Acropolis.

Dionysos, god of wine and drama. It was here at his theatre that the tragedies and comedies by the great fifth century B.C. dramatists had first been performed. These had been produced at the annual Athenian spring festival of the Great Dionysia, where the playwrights of the day competed against one another for a prize. Many of the plays had been about the ancient legends, and had been very popular with the masses, hence the theatre's capacity to seat over seventeen thousand spectators. Tiered seats were hewn out of the Acropolis rock above which the Parthenon stood dominant and resplendant. Marble seats with backs to them for V.I.P.s lined the front row, the one in the centre facing the marble altar being the one reserved for the priest of Dionysos.

The Great Dionysia festival had always started with a spectacular procession in which the statue of Dionysos had been carried on a chariot, and brought to his sanctuary. Dionysos had been regarded as a dying god who, not unlike Demeter's daughter Persephone, returned annually. Maybe the Easter procession of the Epitaphios on Good Friday was a continuation of the Great Dionysia, as the latter was also celebrated in the spring.

We sat on the rock-hewn seats, and looked down at the area where the ancient dramas had been performed. When I remarked to Harry that it was odd that the subject of some plays had been about personal sacrifice in order to redeem people from their sins, and belief in the power of love, and even belief in resurrections, he merely said: "So what?"

"So what?" I regarded Harry. "Because it's interesting that so many Christian ideas were already known four or five hundred years earlier, that's what! For instance, in the play Alcestis by Euripides, Alcestis gave her life for her husband, then returned to life from Hades on the third day! The third day, mind you - not the fifth day, or the second, or tenth, but the third day! And, in another play, the daughter of Agamemnon offers her life as a free sacrifice to save the Greeks as they set off for the Trojan War. In reply to her mother's cries that she'll be lost to her, she says, 'not lost but saved'!"

I thumbed through a book of Greek tragedies I'd brought out with me for the occasion, and found a marked passage from The Bacchae.

"Listen to this," I said, and began to read aloud:

'And is thy Faith so much to give,
Is it so hard a thing to see,
That the Spirit of God, whate'er it be,
The Law that abides and changes not, ages long,
The Eternal and Nature-born - these things be strong?'

"Don't you think that amazing? Those lines were written four hundred and something years B.C. They make God understandable but were referring to pagan gods."

I read the lines again, and tried to imagine the same words being said two and a half thousand years ago when they'd first been unleashed on an attentive audience. When I stopped I was startled by a tap on my shoulder. I turned to find a man and woman seated behind me leaning forward. The man had a neat dark beard streaked with grey and must have been in his late sixties. He wore a battered cream Panama and his clothes, though casual, gave him a certain air of distinction.

"Please excuse this interruption, but are you reading from The Bacchae by Euripides?" he asked. He lifted his Panama briefly from his head revealing thick wiry grey hair. "You like my beloved Euripides?" he enquired. He slipped down to sit beside me and asked if he could look at my book.

"After all these centuries his words still carry with them a timeless spirit of truth," I said.

"You are right," he agreed. "Of all the Euripides plays The Bacchae is my favourite."

With an elbow on each knee he thumbed over some pages thoughtfully. He had the air of a man who had time on his hands. I thought he looked Jewish. A woman, whom I took to be his wife, seated herself beside him, and now leaned forward and spoke across him as he turned the pages.

"Are you from England?" she asked.

"Yes." Her face had a quality, a sort of educated beauty about it. "We too are from England. We arrived in Athens yesterday. Coming here is a celebration for us. It is our ruby wedding. I have always wanted to visit Athens and to see these great archaeological sites."

"Ah! Now let me read you this," interrupted her husband.

" 'Tis not for us to reason touching Gods.
Traditions of our fathers, old as time,
We hold : no reasoning shall cast them down, -
No, though of subtlest wit our wisdom spring...' "

He closed the book without speaking. He had a way of looking down the line of his cheek-bone at me, a sort of sideways assessment. I thought he was waiting for me to say something intelligent. Seeing that no words of wisdom were forthcoming, he remarked: "You know, of course, that Euripides went into self-imposed exile to Macedonia?"

His wife was still leaning forward. "It was because the Athenians accused him of being an atheist, of not honouring the gods but believing there was only one god, wasn't that so, Julian?" she asked.

"He was invited to Macedonia by the king - I forget his name."

"Was it Alexander the Great?"

"No, Euripides was earlier, Madeleine." He looked at the back cover of my book. "Ah! Here I have it! Euripides lived around 480 and died 406 B.C. It was King Archelaus of Macedonia who invited him to his court. The king was envious of Athens with her philosophers, her artists and dramatists. He wanted the same for his own court, and when Euripides came it was a great coup for him, I believe."

"Didn't Euripides have a last minute conversion which prompted him to write the play?" I asked.

"You are right," said the man. "The play was his last, and some say his most sublime. He wrote it whilst at Dion, the ancient city near Mt. Olympus. It was, maybe, first performed there."

"Yes, we've been there."

"You have?" He gave me his 'look' which made me feel as if I'd said something spectacular.

"We should visit the place, Madeleine," he remarked to his wife.

"But it was here, Julian, that the play was first

performed, I am sure of it. The play wasn't discovered until after his death. It was his son who entered it for one of the drama festivals, and it won first prize."

"That's tragic," I said. "It's tragic that a great dramatist never lived to see his greatest work performed."

The man said: "The essential point of the drama is that religion cannot be understood by reason, logic or debate, because it is beyond human understanding."

"Something I'm increasingly aware of," I admitted.

"Because you have the intelligence of Euripides?" queried the man with his 'look' which I found absurdly flattering.

Harry thought it time to join in the conversation and said: "My wife's quite ruthless. Whenever we're in Athens she drags me off to watch some totally incomprehensible Greek tragedy - everyone sobbing and groaning. I haven't a clue what's going on."

"My husband's very long-suffering," I admitted.

"He is a fortunate man to have such a charming wife to take him to see a play by one of the Greek dramatists," said the man with subtle innuendo.

"And they all wear masks!" went on Harry, remaining happily oblivious of any passing attraction between me and this new acquaintance.

The Look smiled. "Well, the season for open-air performances is now over, so you have nothing to fear," he remarked.

For a while we sat talking about Greek drama as though we were old friends. Harry, having had his say, was content just to sit. After about ten minutes the Look turned to his wife, and said something. She leaned forward again. "As we are here celebrating our ruby wedding my husband has suggested, and I would very much like it too, that you will be our guests and meet us for a drink this evening?"

"You must come!" said her husband with boyish enthusiasm, dismissing any negative thoughts. "We are meeting up with a young Greek couple, and you will enjoy their company. They are teachers here in Athens and know many things. You will, I think, find them interesting."

"They speak good English," went on the wife, dispelling any fears Harry might have of not understanding the language.

"And they do not wear masks," added the man with another smile at Harry. I expected a sharp protesting prod from him but, as none came and I remained upright and not doubled over by a blow in the back, I said we'd be delighted. The man took a card from his wallet and handed it to me. "This is our name and mobile number. We are meeting at seven o'clock at the café up Lykabettos. It is the only one and you cannot miss it."

"You know Lykabettos?" enquired his wife.

"Yes, we know it," I replied. "Thank you. We'd very much like to come."

When we parted, Harry grumbled: "I don't know why you've let us in for that!"

"I was waiting for you to make an excuse, and you didn't, that's why."

We left the theatre of Dionysos, and made our way around the Acropolis to the Areópagus, a steep rocky hillock to the north-west. It was there that those accused of blasphemy had once been tried. Uneven and slippery steps were hewn into the rock and were the only means of climbing up. A bronze plaque beside the steps announced that it was where St. Paul had been brought for being a 'babbler' and preaching 'foreign divinities'.

I began to climb to the top feeling uncertain how wise it was to attempt it. I knew I could get up but wasn't too sure about getting down. If there was to be divine retribution, this was the ideal moment to teach me not to be hooked on Euripidean drama in preference to the Old and New Testament.

The flat top of the Areópagus was an uneven death-trap to the unwary; and it was difficult to imagine a court of any sort being held up there. It is thought by some that the court might have sat below which made much more sense.

The Areópagus had become a place for criminal trials ever since Orestes had been advised by Apollo to come to seek justice from Athena for his matricide. When Orestes stood trial, those who sat in judgement were divided in their verdict, half declaring him guilty and half not guilty. It was left to the great goddess of wisdom to cast the deciding vote. This drama was the subject of The Eumenides by the fifth century B.C. dramatist Aeschyllus. After much soul-searching and Chorus-speaking, Athena had finally acquitted him. This had so outraged the Furies that they'd had to be placated and, in her wisdom, Athena had promised them their own place of honour nearby. Thus reconciled, they'd become the Eumenides, the kindly ones. Somewhere below the Areópagus is their own sacred spot.

When St. Paul came to Athens the Athenians were totally bewildered by what he preached. They treated him very politely: '...and they took hold of him and brought him to the Areópagus, saying, "May we know what this new teaching is which you present? For you bring some strange things to our ears; we wish to know therefore what these things mean."' (Acts 17:19)

The interesting result of St. Paul's visit was that one out of his only two converts had been Dionysios the Areópagite. I've read that at the time the name Dionysios with the iota in the spelling denoted a devotee of Dionysos the god.

It was the Epicurean and Stoic philosophers, listening to St. Paul's preaching and finding it incomprehensible, who'd brought him to the Areópagus to put forward his religious views. To the far north-west of where we stood there'd been Plato's Academy where philosophers had wandered and discussed the knotty problems of life and death and divine judgement. Plato had written down the ideas and arguments of Socrates, some of which were not so far removed from Christian teaching. Socrates claimed that the soul was set free from the body at death, and the virtuous would go to the Isles of the Blessed, and the ungodly would depart to Tartarus. He'd maintained that the dead would appear for judgement with their bared and naked souls, so that there could be no camouflaging the truth by fine clothes or pretence of any sort.

'All soul is immortal, for that which is ever in motion is immortal...' (Phaedrus: 245c). Socrates also spoke about the prime mover of life. Without such a prime mover the whole universe, he insisted, 'would collapse into immobility, and never find another source of motion to bring it back into being.' (Phaedrus: 245e). Unlike Euripides, who'd gone into self-imposed exile because he'd rejected the many gods, Socrates had been tried, found guilty and condemned to death for the same thoughts - something which he'd accepted with equanimity and Christ-like calm.

I could well understand Socrates' view of a prime mover, of an overall eternal spirit, but found it difficult to equate this supreme being with the Jewish God who commanded worship and obedience as a jealous deity, and threatened poor mortals with divine judgement.

"Where do you think thought comes from?" I asked Harry suddenly. We were looking towards the wonderfully preserved Hephaesteion (the temple of Hephaestus) beyond which the Academy of Plato would have been.

"Thought? Well, I suppose from the brain."

"You'd think so. But the brain just gives words to the thought so you can speak it. Or it can just keep the thought to itself and mull it over. What actually puts the thought into your head?"

"I've no idea. Have we got anything to eat?" Harry's own thought at that moment concerned food. I could understand food-thought prompted by hunger; it was the sudden thought regarding an idea, something that came without physical prompting that was strange.

"It's quite frightening to think that a thought comes into your mind from an unseen source," I said. "Can you imagine the air around you absolutely seething with invisible thoughts waiting to gain entry to your head? Or perhaps people are born with inbuilt thoughts which ripen and burst into life on contact with - well, with someone else with similar thoughts?" I thought briefly of the man and his wife we'd just met.

"Never mind thoughts, do we have a knife for the cheese?" Harry had taken two buttered rolls from the haversack.

I could see my great exploration of the mind was going to get nowhere, and found a knife in a side pocket of the haversack.

"How's the thumb?" Harry enquired, seeing me use my unbandaged hand to unzip the pocket.

Vision prompting a thought was also quite understandable. "Well, it's not throbbing or anything. But I'm not going to unbandage it to look," I answered.

"Absolutely not. Well, after a few days perhaps you should."

All thoughts were, I supposed, generated from vision, feelings, upbringing, education - But the thoughts that led to a mystery cult in religion and worship, where did they come from? The day before, on the morning of Agios Dionysios' feast-day, I'd got up early and visited the cathedral where a liturgy had been underway. The bishop had been officiating wearing his tall black head-dress with long black veil behind, and scarlet and gold robes. The choir of four men on either side had been chanting, and a priest had stood in the ornate pulpit holding up the Gospels for all to see. All this was part of ritual; but what thoughts had first created this ritual? What had inspired the thoughts?

The interior of the cathedral had looked far more attractive than I'd remembered it from previous occasions. I didn't recall having ever seen the opaque engraved glass of the Royal Doors to the iconostasis. When the bishop had entered the sanctuary there'd been a shadowy image of him through the Royal Doors being divested of his headgear and being re-robed - a sort of Socratean image when only a shadowy part of the true facts could be detected by the mere human eye and mind. Having watched the dignity of the liturgy unfold that morning, I imagined that, in order to civilize the mortal world, it had been necessary to channel thoughts to the higher and the better, and away from the evil influences capable of destroying the common good. It had been important to give flesh and blood to the abstract idea of virtue, and turn the human mind towards a godly figure. Socrates had been convinced that 'Love will help our mortal nature more than all the world. And this is why I say that every man of us should worship the god of love, and this is why I cultivate and worship all the elements of Love myself, and bid others do the same.' (Plato's Symposium: 212b).

By now we'd finished our picnic, and Harry was getting restless. To descend the rock-hewn steps looked like an invitation to break a leg. We removed our sandals so that our bare feet would have more grip on the slippery well-worn steps. Harry went first, and I played the helpless-woman-with-a-bandaged-thumb act, and got the assistance of a young man's arm to help me lower myself step by slippery step, and more on my behind than on my feet, to the ground below. If I was to be clobbered by a divine hand then the descent from the Areópagus, where criminals and blasphemers had been tried, was the most obvious place for it. But once again I was spared such a fate.

"Was Greece top of your list?" I asked.

"It was top of my list," the Look's wife interjected, turning briefly from Harry. She was seated beside him and I noticed that, whilst paying hostess-like attention to him, she also had the ability to catch what others were saying around the table. Certainly she knew what I was saying to her husband, or what he was saying to me.

The party was in full swing and, as she and her husband had said, the two young Greeks were charming; there was an energy and spontaneity about them which was infectious. The young man was well built and serious faced, and his fiancée was an attractive, lively thirty year old with shoulder-length dark hair. They were both teachers, he of history and she of languages, and both were fluent in English.

Conversation had at first ranged around their lives, before moving on to our lives, and finally fixing on the more metaphysical subject of being alive at all. I'd learned from the Look that his parents had been Jewish immigrants from Lithuania, and he'd trained as a doctor ending up as a hospital surgeon. Now in his retirement he intended to fulfil his lifelong dream of seeing the ancient civilizations of the world.

"And after Greece I am keen to visit Egypt - Mesopotamia - China - " he remarked. At the mention of each country he raised his head higher and higher, as he assessed me down the line of his cheek-bone. He and his wife were well dressed for their evening party, whilst we had only improvised with a clean shirt for Harry, and a chiffon scarf for me tossed nonchalantly over one shoulder, the best I could do when travelling light. "When you are dealing daily with patients who are near to death," went on the Look, "you realize the good fortune of having good health. Good health gives you the opportunity to fulfil your dreams."

"What's the secret of good health?" I asked.

"You always tell me good health is a well balanced mind, Julian," put in his wife.

"I agree that a well balanced mind helps. And I would say contentment also."

"Does contentment come from being well balanced?" I asked, trying to keep up the expectations the Look had of me, and wondering how much longer I could keep up being reasonably intelligent. So far the wine hadn't gone to my head but was helping to get me going.

Athens lay spread-eagled before us in a panoramic arc of twinkling lights hemmed in by the mountains to the east and west. In the near distance was the Acropolis, a dark silhouette and sombre shadow in the twilight. The city reminded me of an overturned wide-lipped bowl spilling its contents down to the port of Piraeus. An occasional ferry-boat or cruise liner festooned with fairy lights sailed into the far distant harbour.

Soon the discussion was in full swing regarding the phenomenon of the human body, and its remarkable and infinitely complicated construction. It was a subject which led to the topic that Harry and I disagreed profoundly about regarding the Darwin theory of evolution, mutation and the survival of the fittest. Harry favoured Darwin, but I couldn't for a moment accept that human beings or animals of different species, each with their remarkably complex make-up, could have mutated to their present forms without dying first because of some malfunction.

"I keep telling my poor wife it took millions of years," said Harry, convinced that his own point of view, influenced by Darwin, could be the only correct one.

The Look's wife sided with Harry, the young couple also, whilst the Look himself listened but remained silent.

"How," I demanded, "could a sudden mutation meet with another fellow mutation to reproduce a mutated offspring? And anyway, how did male and female first separate out and get the urge to procreate?"

"We're talking billions of years!" Harry insisted, doubling up on the original millions as if it answered my question.

"All right," I said, "you say it took billions of years but! - if I was wanting to make a profoundly complicated piece of machinery, or any bit of machinery for that matter, then billions and billions of years would never just by chance or coincidence bring the necessary pieces together to make that perfect bit of machinery. It just has to have a mind of sorts at work to assemble it. There just has to be!"

"Ah! So you believe in God's creation!" exclaimed the Look.

"I believe in a Holy Spirit of creation," I corrected.

"Not the Jewish story of creation?" he enquired.

"The Genesis story is one of many creation stories," I said. "Do you believe in it?"

"As you say, it's a story. I accept the part where God breathed the breath of life into his first man."

"A Holy Spirit of sorts?" I asked.

"So we agree on that point?"

"We agree on that point."

"My wife thinks she's an unbeliever. But she believes really," said Harry.

"In my experience it is easier to believe than not to believe," interjected the Look's wife.

"She was nearly killed by a motorbike yesterday," remarked Harry with a note of pride, as though he'd been the one who'd saved me from death.

I held up my bandaged thumb as evidence. "I thought I'd lost an arm but I only had a gash on the end of my thumb."

"Then you were lucky."

"How did it happen?" asked the girl.

After telling them the circumstances, I went on: "But to get back to the wonders of the body! Isn't it amazing how it can repair itself? Don't you find that remarkable?"

"Ah! That is another thing we can agree on," said the Look.

By now the wine had not only got me going but I was

unstoppable. "To think of the body's fantastic ability to self-repair itself! To think of its capacity to be healthy! Take the digestive system as an example. Take the function of the kidneys, the liver, the everything to do with digestion. Take, for example, the incredible detail of the jaw and throat - the minutely balanced quantity of saliva in the mouth and on the tongue and the gums. And I haven't even mentioned the nervous system, the eyes, the ears, the brain!" I put out my hand and rotated my wrist and bent my fingers and displayed my bandaged thumb. "The incredible versatility of the hand alone is quite amazing. The nails, the veins, the ligaments, the bones - and the gash on the end of my thumb quietly repairing itself. Isn't that all astonishing? The human body and mind cannot, just cannot be the result of mutation!"

"The subject is so complex," said the Look, "that nobody can fully grasp the phenomenon of human life. The brain and mind together has not the capacity and can only speculate. I agree, it is remarkable."

When the subject was exhausted, I turned to the young couple and told them how I loved Greece, its old gods and legends, and how I found the archaeological sites fascinating as they appeared to be built on locations known to have sacred qualities.

"Of course!" the young man said. He tended to reply to anything I said with 'Of course!' "Of course!" he said, "the Greek people are always aware of the sacred and the spiritual. In my opinion nothing is truly changed from before Christianity."

"What do you mean by that?" I asked.

The young man answered vigorously: "You have to understand that here in Greece it is not for Christianity that the people come to the church, they come for the mystery."

"For the mystery?" I asked in surprise.

"Of course! Everybody he likes the mystery. You cannot explain it in black or in white or in easy sentences. The more you try to explain Christianity the more difficult it is to understand."

"Our people," began the fiancée, "are happy with the customs of our land. Have you ever been to Greece for Easter? It is a big celebration of the mystery - the mystery of life and death and life again. To me it is like the old tragedies. The people come to watch the actors who play the part in the tragedy. Some characters in the play they die, and others they lament and the audience weeps for them. All take part and are involved, but at the same time they know they are only acting or observing the tragedy. It is a kind of mirror-image that takes place. It is very interesting."

"Of course!" cried the young man. "The people go to church at this time, not just for the Resurrection as I believe is the custom for you in England, but for each day of Holy Week. It is a tradition from ancient times when the festivals they go on for three or four days. It is difficult to break such a custom. People want festivals to release them from their work, from the worries - from the wife!" He nudged his fiancée playfully.

"From the husband!" she retorted with as much spirit.

She turned back towards me and said: "I think you are interested in our Greek philosophers? In Socrates and Plato and Aristotle?" She looked at me enquiringly. "I think you are interested when I tell you that even then, three, four hundred years before Christ, they talk much about the gods, and with their brains and their logic they work out that there is only one God?"

"They say that there is Zeus who is the great god and all the others - "

"Eventually became saints?" I prompted.

"Of course!" cried the young man. "It is all part of the big mystery. The people do not like to lose altogether the ancient mysteries of their gods, so they make them the saints and servants of Jesus Christ."

"The Holy Spirit is something I can understand very well," I said. "The holy breath of life, or Agion Pneuma," I said in Greek.

"Of course! The mystery is everywhere with us, every moment of every day!"

"That is true," said the fiancée, "but most people they are too busy with their lives to think about these things. Many use the Church because they are superstitious."

"It is as St. Paul once said, that the people of Athens are a very 'superstitious people'. I think you have it in translation that they are a very 'religious people'. But the word in the Greek New Testament is 'superstitious', not 'religious'."

"Not forgetting," said our hostess, "and I find many Christians do forget this - that Jesus was a Jew."

"And St. Paul also was a Jew." said the Look. "And the Apostles were all Jews. All were believers of the same God - a supreme deity, an eternal omnipotent power."

I was captivated by the moment, when the strings of doctrinal belief were being untied, and the immensity of the subject was being allowed to manifest itself. Harry listened with a smiling countenance as the young couple enthusiastically continued the discussion. The young man put an arm around the shoulders of his fiancée as he went on: "Life is a great drama - it is the story of Demeter whose daughter was abducted at Eleusis; it is the tragedy of Aphrodite and her beloved Adonis who was killed as a young man; it is the jealousy of Hera due to the unfaithfulness of Zeus."

"But you must not forget, Nikos, the joys of life. You must remember also that life is the joy of music with Apollo; of literature and inspiration with the Muses; the hunting with Artemis."

"The love of Aphrodite!"

"And the love of Aphrodite!" she agreed from the depth of his arm. "You have the happiness but also its opposite with sadness. This is something Socrates knew about."

"The Greeks identify themselves with all these stories as well as with Jesus Christ who the Church tells us was crucified and rose from the dead. Nobody says you have to believe it. But you must understand that as a mystery it draws people together in sorrow and then in joy and hope."

I was delighted with what they said. It was so unexpected that it was almost as though God, or the gods themselves, had arranged the evening for me.

Before we parted I had taken the young couple's name and address in order to keep in touch. Names and addresses were exchanged with the Look and his wife also. Once the Look had kissed my hand (which I thought incredibly romantic) and he and his wife had disappeared into the night, Harry said: "Well, that's that! Funny fellow! Came from Lithuania or Latvia or one of these suspect places." He stood up. "Thank God, this time tomorrow we'll be home again!"

The wine and the effort of keeping intelligent all evening made me feel suddenly quite drained and, instead of moving, I stayed rooted to my chair. The night was warm and there was a half moon hanging in the sky above the Parthenon which was now flood-lit. In fact, there were two half moons and several Parthenons.

"Suffering from delayed shock?" Harry asked. He peered at me almost with the same attention as the Look. "I warned you you might suffer from that."

After a cup of strong black coffee, and I was seeing one half moon and one Parthenon again, it suddenly struck me that, thanks to the young Greeks that evening, there was no need any more to look for solutions to impossible-to-answer questions. It always was and always would remain a mystery.

The flood-lit Parthenon rose against the night sky in all its ancient majesty and beauty, a lasting symbol of these strange, eternal and unfathomable secrets.

THE END

GLOSSARY OF GODS & HEROES

ACHILLES

Son of Peleus and Thetis, and Greek hero of the Trojan War. He was furious when King Agamemnon stole his slave girl and, as a consequence, refused to fight. Only when the Greeks were on the point of defeat and his best friend Patroclus was killed, did he consent to rejoin the battle and, by his strength and valour, brought victory to the Greeks.

AEGISTHUS

Seducer of Clytemnestra, wife of King Agamemnon. He helped Clytemnestra murder her husband on his return from the Trojan War.

AGAMEMNON

King of Mycenae and leader of the Achaeans (Greeks) in the Trojan War. He was murdered by his wife, Clytemnestra, on his return.

ALEXANDER THE GREAT

(356-323 B.C.) King of Macedonia, son of Philip II and Olympias. He was a keen admirer of Homer's Iliad and carried a copy of it with him throughout his campaigns.

AMPHITRITE

Wife of Poseidon.

APHRODITE

Goddess of love.

APOLLO

Son of Zeus and Leto, and twin brother of Artemis. He was god of music, archery and prophecy.

ARES
God of war.

ARGUS
A herdsman who had eyes all over his body. Hera put him to watch over her priestess, Io, when Zeus became enamoured of her.

ARTEMIS
Daughter of Zeus and Leto, and twin sister of Apollo. She was goddess of wild life and hunting.

ASCLEPIUS
God of medicine, son of Apollo and a mortal woman.

ATHENA
Daughter of Zeus. She was virgin goddess of wisdom, arts and crafts.

BELLEROPHON
A courageous young man who, like Hercules, performed many labours which were intended to test him to the limit.

CENTAURS
Strange beings who were half horse, half man.

CHARON
The ferryman who rowed the dead across the river Styx to Hades.

CHIRON
A Centaur who was both wise and kind and knowledgeable in music, archery and medicine.

CLYTEMNESTRA
Wife of Agamemnon, king of Mycenae, and sister of Helen of Troy. Clytemnestra murdered her husband on his return from the Trojan War.

COSMAS and DAMIAN

Two early Christian saints, patron saints of physicians. They were popularly known as the penniless ones because they would take no money for their services. In the fifth or sixth century a large Byzantine church, believed to have been dedicated to these two healing saints, was built in the sanctuary of Asclepius, god of healing, south of the Acropolis in Athens.

CYCLOPES

One-eyed giants who made thunderbolts for Zeus.

DAPHNE

A nymph who was pursued by Apollo until her mother, Gaea, turned her into a bay or laurel tree.

DEMETER

Goddess of corn and agriculture.

DIONYSOS

Son of Zeus and a mortal woman. He was god of wine and drama.

EURYDICE

A beautiful nymph who married Orpheus and died tragically soon afterwards from a snake bite.

FATES

See Moirai.

FURIES

Greek spirits of vengeance who harassed those who committed murder, especially within a family. They were often portrayed as winged women, and could be regarded as symbolizing pangs of conscience.

GAEA

Personification of the earth.

GLAUKE

Jason's second wife who was sent a poisoned garment by Medea (his jealous first wife). When she put it on she immediate caught fire and was burned to death.

HADES

Brother of Zeus and god of the underworld.

HELEN

The beautiful wife of Menelaus, king of Sparta. She was seduced by Paris and ran away with him to Troy which triggered the Trojan War.

HEPHAESTUS

Lame son of Zeus and Hera. He was god of fire and a master craftsman in all metal work.

HERA

Wife of Zeus, goddess of women and marriage.

HERCULES

Best known of the Greek heroes for his twelve labours. He was renowned for his courage, strength, endurance and compassion.

HERMES

A messenger of the gods. He conducted the souls of the dead to Hades.

HESTIA

Goddess of the hearth, symbol of the home and family.

HIPPODAMEIA

Ill-gotten wife of Pelops who bribed, cheated and murdered in order to marry her.

HIPPOLYTUS

Son of Theseus and the Amazon queen, Hippolyta, with whom Theseus' second wife, Phaedra, fell hopelessly in love with disastrous consequences.

HYGIEA

Daughter of Asclepius, god of medicine.

IACCHOS

A little known god who was identified with Dionysos, and played a part in the Eleusinian Mysteries.

IO

A priestess at the Heraion, Argos, with whom Zeus fell in love. Hera in her anger changed Io into a heifer and set a gadfly on her which chased her all over the world.

JASON

The rightful heir to the throne of a kingdom in Thessaly, northern Greece. Before he could claim it, however, he had to recover the golden fleece.

KORE

See Persephone.

KRONOS

Married to Rhea. He was father of Zeus and many other Olympian deities.

LETO

Mother of Apollo and Artemis by Zeus.

MEDEA

An enchantress who fell in love with Jason. With the help of her magic, Jason was able to recover the golden fleece and, therefore, his kingdom.

MEDUSA

One of the Gorgons. They were all hideous with glaring eyes and snakes around their heads for hair.

MENELAUS

King of Sparta, married to Helen who ran off with Paris to Troy.

MOIRAI

The Fates. Three in number: the first assigned man's lot at birth, the second spun the thread of life, and the third cut it at death.

MUSES

Nine daughters of Zeus and Mnemosyne (personification of Memory). Each presided over one of the arts or sciences.

NEREIDS

Sea maidens.

NIKE

The Greek personification of victory.

ODYSSEUS

A hero of the Trojan War in Homer's Illiad, and The Odyssey. He is courageous, resourceful and able to overcome crises.

OLYMPIAS

Mother of Alexander the Great.

ORESTES

Son of King Agamemnon and Clytemnestra. He was hounded by the Furies after he killed his mother in order to avenge her murder of his father.

ORPHEUS

Founder of the mystic cult of Orphism. He was the son of one of the Muses and possibly Apollo, and became renowned for charming wild beasts with his singing. He married Eurydice and was distraught when she died soon afterwards from a snake bite.

PANACEA

Daughter of Asclepius, god of medicine.

PARIS

Son of the King of Troy. Aphrodite helped him to seduce the beautiful Helen which triggered the Trojan War.

PEGASUS

A winged horse believed to have sprung from the blood of Medusa when her head was cut off.

PEIRENE

Daughter of a river god, who was loved by Poseidon and gave birth to a son. When the son died she wept so much she turned into a spring.

PELEUS

King of Thessaly, married to Thetis, a Nereid. Achilles was their son.

PELOPS

A young man who by treachery won for his bride the King of Elis' daughter, Hippodameia. This evil brought a curse down on their descendents. King Agamemnon was their grandson.

PERSEPHONE

Daughter of Demeter. She was a beautiful young goddess who was abducted and carried off to the underworld by Hades and became his queen.

PHAEDRA

Wife of Theseus who fell in love with Hippolytus, her step-son, with tragic consequences.

POSEIDON

Brother of Zeus. He was god of the sea as well as of earthquakes and horses.

PYTHIA

The priestess of Apollo at Delphi through whom the god gave his oracles.

PYTHON

A monstrous serpent (or dragoness, according to Homer) who inhabited Delphi before Apollo came and slew it.

RHEA

Wife of Kronos and mother of Zeus and many other Olympians.

SILENI

Sons of Silenus. They all had snub noses and the tail and ears of a horse; they were also bald and pot-bellied, and frequently fell in love with Nymphs. They joined in the revels of Dionysos, god of wine and drama.

SIRENS

Weird women who lured sailors to their doom by their singing.

THEMIS

Mother of the Fates.

THESEUS

Legendary King of Athens.

THETIS

A sea-nymph, married to Peleus. Their son was Achilles. To make him immortal Thetis held him by the heel in the river Styx. Where she gripped him, however, remained for ever mortal - hence the saying someone has an 'Achilles heel', a vulnerable spot.

TIRESIAS

A man who, unfortunately, caught sight of Athena bathing naked and was blinded as a consequence. To compensate him Athena granted him the gift of prophecy.

TROJAN WAR

A war waged by the Achaeans (Greeks) against the Trojans in order to recover Helen who had run off with Paris, son of the King of Troy.

ZEUS

Supreme god of the ancient world. God of the heavens and controller of the weather. In classical times he was regarded as protector of civic law and justice.

REVIEWS OF 'HOLY SMOKE!'

'It is Jill's stance as "agnostic but quite religious" that marks out her travel writing as something special...

Holy Smoke! is another winning work, with her sceptical forays again entertainingly set off against her husband Harry, who takes Christianity on trust.'

Western Daily Press

'Holy Smoke! is an account of Jill's travels through Turkey and Egypt between the 9/11 tragedy and war in Iraq. In search of answers to questions posed by the religious beliefs of Christians, Jews and Moslems, she takes the reader on a fascinating journey through facts and legends... down Anatolia to the Aegean and around Egypt...'

Marshwood Vale Magazine

JILL DUDLEY'S
NEXT BOOK

'MORTALS & IMMORTALS'
THE GREEK GODS VISIT BRITAIN

A SATIRICAL FANTASY
& TRUE-IN-PARTS MEMOIR